A WARRIOR CULTURE

Surrounding Yourself with Dangerous Men of God

Donny Prater

Dedications

Marci- Thank you for allowing me to be your warrior.

Will – God's mighty warrior in the making.

My Warrior Culture of Brothers

Forward

In the last few years, the Church is becoming more and more aware of a Christian Men's Movement. All over the world men are being spurred on to accept their role as men in the Church, home, and in the life circles God has placed them. This masculine awakening has gained much of its ground through men specific studies that have sprung up through "grassroots" movements. Unfortunately, many women, without knowing the whole story, may disregard them as some weird male bonding experiment or discount it as misspent testosterone. But from what I've seen, the face of the Church is finally starting to change for the better when it comes to the spirituality of its men.

All over the world men are waking up to a revived relationship with Christ and in better touch with their masculinity. Although this is refreshing, the fact remains that some men get it and some don't. I've seen men come alive in Christ and become great warriors that change lives and affect generations to come. But on the flip side, I've seen men go out and buy a Harley because that's what they felt God was telling them to do. By writing this book, I know I will step on some toes, make some people blush, and even infuriate a few. If I didn't accomplish all of those, I would count it a waste of my time. All of that said, at the end of the day, it is worth it to see men grasp the concept that they desperately need other warriors to fight alongside of, all the while forming life-long bonds that the gates of hell cannot overcome. That is what this world needs, passionate and dangerous men that are ready to fight at a moments notice, and take back what has been stolen by the Enemy.

By the grace of God, I have found myself right in the middle of this movement and have seen what the power of God can do in the lives of men. God gave me a burden for helping men grow in Christ many years ago and I know the words of this book were written on my heart the day He created me. My prayer for you is that you will use this book as a resource to help you build a group of warriors that will surround you, fight for you, and take ground for the Kingdom.

Let me assure you that by reading this book, you are about to embark on a journey with me as your guide The first thing you do before taking a journey is make sure you've packed the right gear. The neat thing about this journey is, if your name is already written in the Lamb's Book of Life, you are ready to push off. If you have any doubts about where you stand with God, there is a simple childlike prayer that you can say right now and mean it in your heart that is essential to your journey. That prayer is:

> Dear Lord Jesus, I believe you died and rose again to pay for my sins. I receive you into my heart to reside as my savior. I put all of my faith in you and ask you to become the master of my life. Amen

If you prayed that prayer and meant it, welcome home! Hold on to your saddle horn, here we go!

Table of Contents

Introduction

It was 6:00 AM on a Saturday in May as I drove to the Church. As the Men's Ministry Leader, I had to be there in time to cook the pancakes and sausage, set the tables, make the coffee, and be sure the biscuits went into the oven on time. I was expecting a good turnout of men for our time of fellowship and was looking forward to hearing our Pastor give a devotional. What could be better than eating and learning God's word with a group of men?

When 8:00 AM rolled around, the men began to trickle in, exercising the usual handshake and a smile with on another. By 8:30 there were twenty-five men divided into six smaller groups and having their own individual coffee-clutch meetings. It was time to eat so I welcomed everyone, gave the blessing, and the feeding began.

About fifteen minutes into my meal, I started noticing men heading out the door as soon as they were finished eating. This struck me as funny and I wondered what they were up to. I kept noticing man after man throw away their garbage and file out the door. By 9:00, I was faced with the reality that out of twenty-five men, only five remained. I grabbed the Pastor and asked him, "Where did everybody go?" He told me he wasn't sure but he figured it had something to do with cutting grass. I headed for the door, searching for some answers and I came face to face with one of my well-fed Christian Brothers. Before I had a chance to speak, he asked me, "Donny do you know if there is any orange juice? I want to get hydrated before I start pushing the mower around."

By now, I was fuming. What I had planned for this morning was not only a time of fellowship and food but also a way to introduce how we were going to kick start our Men's Ministry. I was prepared to pour my heart out to these men in hopes of finding some takers that would be willing to become part of a men's leadership group. Instead, what it had turned into was a free breakfast for everyone prior to their work day at Church.

That was the turning point for me as a Men's Ministry Leader. I started praying to God and asking him to reveal to me what I should do next. He guided me to spend the next two years reading and researching why men are the way they are. I didn't see any reason to break from the norm so we continued to have the same old empty breakfasts and dinner times of fellowship that got us nowhere. Through my time of study and prayer, an amazing thing began to happen. God started equipping me with the knowledge that I have presented in this book and things started to change for the better in the Men's Ministry at my Church.

First, God sent me helpers that had a passion for helping men and a core group was formed. This core group formed a leadership team chaired by a Church Elder that went on to organize, build, and develop a revolutionary style of Men's Ministry that is based upon building relationships and relying on each other. This is by far a departure from the norm for most Churches that are stuck in the rut that revolves around pancake breakfasts and golf outings.

If you find yourself stuck in a similar rut, this book is for you. But before you begin, remember that dynamics differ from Church to Church and everything I present here may not work in your situation. However, the basic fact is that it is high time that men unite as warriors, pick up their swords, and most of all exercise them for the Kingdom.

Chapter 1
The Enemy Prowls

The lion is the quintessential symbol of strength, majesty, ferociousness, stealth, destruction, and power. By far, when God created him, he must have known he had just crafted the king of the beasts. Let's face it, he is the biggest kid on the block, especially if your block is the savannah. An adult male lion stands up to 5 feet tall is 9 feet in length and can weigh up to 450 pounds. The lion can run at speeds up to 38 mph can leap up to 12 feet vertically and 36 feet horizontally. Armed with powerful legs, he can snap a zebra's vertebrae in one swipe and his massive jaws can sever a spinal cord in one bite. The eyes of the lion are six times more powerful than human eyes, which gives him the capability of night vision. Lions are also fitted with sensitive ears that can hear prey up to a mile away. With all of these features, I hope you can clearly see that there is no other animal on earth better suited for killing than the lion.

The lion lacks little in physical ability and is equally impressive with its mental prowess. A hunting lion is the most patient and calculating killer on earth and implores the most ruthless, yet scientific methods for catching game. Prior to hunting, the pride will divide into an attack group made up of the fastest and strongest animals and an ambush group that is normally comprised of the younger apprentice cats and females. Members of the attack group use their inherent stealthiness to get as close as possible to an unsuspecting herd of animals. It may take hours for the hunting party to creep into position so that they can observe the unsuspecting prey. From their covert positions, the lions will size up the entire herd and identify the weakest animal of the group. This process of elimination may take hours but is crucial to the battle plan. Once the pride has marked their target, the attack begins.

The attack group will charge the herd and cause great confusion and panic. As if herding sheep, the attacking lions will drive the herd toward the ambush group that lies in wait, ready to spring the trap. Once the herd reaches the ambush group, the lions flank the herd and isolate the animal that has been marked for death. The isolated animal has lost it's only defense (strength in numbers) and will run into a dead end. There is no escaping a pack of hungry lions that have picked you to be their dinner guest.

A group of hungry lions will carry out the dance of death by first jumping onto the prey's back and sinking their mighty claws deep into the animals flesh. In most cases, after several lions have latched onto the animal's back, the largest male lion will normally take the supreme duty of clamping onto the neck, crushing the esophagus. Most times, the lion will suffocate the animal, but if the pride is hungry enough they will simply rip the animal to shreds and devour it while its heart is still beating. On the savannah, survival of the fittest and sacrifice of the weakest is a common part of everyday life.

The instinct of the lion cannot be eclipsed by any other animal when it comes to the way that it hunts. In fact, many African tribesmen believe that the lion possesses the supernatural ability to enter the thoughts of their prey and make the killing easier. Tribesmen also believe that the lion can communicate with other members of its pride simply by thinking thoughts in an unexplained telepathic method. I'm not sure if I believe this myth, but the lion's demonstration of power does make a good case on its behalf.

The lion is an animal to be feared not only because of its well known power but also because it is a patient killer that sizes up the prey before attacking. It is no wonder that when the apostle Peter referred to our Enemy, he said:

> "Be controlled and alert, Your enemy
> the devil prowls around like a roaring **lion**
> looking for someone to devour." -1 Peter 5:8

What Peter was trying to tell us is that we have a very real and a very powerful enemy that seeks to kill us. This enemy is roaming around us at all times, looking for a weakness, and waiting for the appropriate time to isolate us, and sink his claws into our flesh. This Enemy of our souls may use the same tactics as the lion, but comparing him to a lion is like comparing a fuzzy teddy bear to an angry grizzly bear. He is powerful and you must accept the fact that he is as real as the hair on your head. If you reject the fact that he is real and is out to ambush you, you are already held firmly in his grip. But who is this of which we speak? His name is Satan and he commands a massive army of fallen angels.

But, who is Satan and what is his story? The Bible describes Satan as the "deceiver" and the "father of lies". Other names for him that are found in scripture are the adversary, slanderous, fierce, deceitful, cowardly, and wicked. Let's face it he is the most evil being in the universe and despises all things good, pure, and holy. But it wasn't always that way. Satan was once a marvelous creature and could even be described as the apple of God's eye.

When we look into Satan's beginning, we do not see a hideous or even a scary being. Instead, we find that Satan was the perfect picture of beauty crafted by the hand of God. It may be hard for you to picture this, but Satan was once the prized possession of God. The prophet Ezekiel described Satan as, "The anointed cherub that God created to cover his throne" (Ez 28:14). It is no doubt that Satan was the most beautiful, powerful and favored by God among angels. But what went wrong? Or better yet how did he go from blessed to cursed? The answer to this question can be found in the principle of free will.

The mystery of why God gave angels and men free will to choose him or reject him is just that, a great mystery. However, He is God and He created angels and men as free spirits with the ability to choose between good and evil. What happened was simple, pride was born! Satan enjoyed his status so much that he grew power hungry. His thirst for power soon created a vacuum inside him that was filled with pride. The Prophet Isaiah spoke of the prideful vanity of Satan when he wrote:

> "I will ascend into heaven, I will exalt my throne above the stars of God....I will be like the most High" (Is 14:13-14)..

Satan in essence, fell in love with himself, turned against God, and in so doing, tried to become God. I cannot fathom what was going through his mind when he chose this path. I also cannot imagine the pain God experienced when his prized creation turned on him.

Satan's plan to overthrow God began when he used his other inherent trait of deception on the angels. He was obviously the greatest salesman ever created because he managed to convince a third of all the angels in heaven to follow him and deny God. He should have known he was outnumbered and outgunned but he was blinded by pride and could not see the awesome power of God. As I have seen in my own life, pride has a way of blinding you to the point you can convince yourself of anything, no matter how far fetched, as long as the potential outcome will glorify you.

As you can imagine, Satan's attempt to over-throw God resulted in a tumultuous war in heaven. It is beyond our simple human minds to imagine the violence and raw brutality that was exhibited during that epic struggle. In short, Satan lost and was cast out of heaven along with all of his angel army. The bad news for us is that he was cast down to Earth where he is known as:

"Prince of the power of the air" (Eph 2:2)

and

"the god of this world" (II Cor 4:4)

So, if you haven't thought much about it, you live in the realm of Satan. This is his world and his kingdom you were born into. We live on his turf where he spends his days commanding his powerful army to wage war against you **ONLY** to steal from you, kill you, and utterly destroy everything associated with you (John 10:10).

Warring against man is his specialty that he has perfected through time. Satan's methods of attack are much like the lion in that he patiently calculates your weaknesses with stealthy precision prior to attack. He seeks to isolate you from the pack and pounce on you. Some of his methods of attack that are docu-mented in scripture include:

He relies on disguise - "And no wonder, for Satan himself masquerades as an angel of light" (II Cor 11:14)

He insinuates doubt – "Now the serpent was more crafty than any of the wild animals the Lord God had made. He said to the woman, "Did God really say, 'You must not eat from any tree in the garden'?" (Gen 3:1)

He misuses and misquotes scripture – "If you are the Son of God," he said, "throw yourself down. For it is written: "'He will command his angels concerning you, and they will lift you up in their hands, so that you will not strike your foot against a stone.'" (Matt 4:6)

He devises schemes – "in order that Satan might not outwit us. For we are not unaware of his schemes." (II Cor 2:11)

As soon as God created Adam, you better believe Satan was plotting and planning his first attack. How dare God create something to take his place? In Genesis we find that he did a great job in his first area of operation, the Garden of Eden. He pulled it off in a big way in the garden by first deceiving Eve, who handed the fruit to Adam (who was right there with her the whole time and stood silent), he ate it, and thus occurred the fall of man. Satan learned right then and there that if he approaches us the right way and tweaks the story to get us interested, we will believe him. It worked on us back then and it still works today. Satan must be a firm believer in one of my Dad's favorite sayings, "If it ain't broke, don't fix it".

I've been asked before "Why does he pick on us?". Well, think about this: man was created in the image of the Most High God. We are the walking and talking copies of the one entity that Satan detests and envies more than anything else. His hatred for us also burns because we were created for the sole purpose of pleasing God and also as an outlet for Him to channel His amazing love. Each one of us were created to love and worship God for all the days of our lives. Satan is jealous.

Satan also knows that God hates to be separated from his children. His ultimate goal is to make sure that we live a life without God and ultimately die sending our soul to spend eternity without God. That is his goal, totally isolating you from God!

To understand the principle behind why Satan wars against us, we also need to see things through the eyes of John the Revelator. In Revelations 12:17, he wrote:

> "The dragon was enraged at the woman and went off to **make war** against the rest of her offspring – those who obey God's commandments and hold to the testimony of Jesus." (Rev 12:17)

So guess what, he's gunning for you, me, and every other child of the King. If you think about it, the Enemy has sunk to the lowest of lows. Since he could not defeat God, he has decided to take it out on His children. Whether a person is a Christian or not, he or she is still an heir to a grand inheritance from God. The Enemy hates this fact because he wants the inheritance for himself (he tried to take it by force and failed) and his jealousy drives his hatred.

I can tell you beyond a shadow of a doubt that if someone attacked my son because they did not like me, I would consider it the lowest form of attack and would be ready to fight tooth and nail. It is no different in the eyes of God. In the greatest form of passion ever exhibited, God sent his only son Jesus (the Word) to die for us and give everyone the opportunity to come to him through his son. In so doing, he also gave us permission to use the name of Jesus to protect ourselves. The Bible tells us:

"Resist the Devil and he will flee from you" (James 4:7)

"For the Word of God is sharper than any double-edged sword, it penetrates even to dividing soul and spirit, joints and marrow. It judges the thoughts and attitudes of the heart." (Heb 4:12)

The Enemy and his goons must leave you alone when you demand it in the name of Jesus, we've got God's word on it. So child of God, what you are faced with are two choices; fight or compromise. I comprised once and paid the price.

I went through a season in my life in which I had let God breathe new life into me. I was on fire for the Lord and it sprang from my involvement with a powerful circle of true men of God. We prayed together, encouraged each other daily, and met together in a small group every week. In this small group, we opened up and revealed things about ourselves that we would have never let anyone else in on. We fought for each other and received healing for our own personal faults. This was the closest to God I had ever been.

Then, it happened. I told my brothers that I would have to miss a couple of weeks because I had a schedule conflict. Two weeks passed, then another two and before you know it I had taken myself out of the group. My brothers were continually calling me and letting me know about the prayers they were lifting up for me, but I was finding comfort in being out of the group. I didn't realize it at the time but I was isolated and slowly suffocating. My pride would not allow me to return to the group out of fear that it would only show my weakness.

I stayed out of the group for about three months. Then, out of the blue, my warrior brother Randy dropped the atomic bomb on me in the form of an email. This email ripped me up one side and down the other and told me to get over myself and get back in. He wrote:

"You are isolated and cut off from the pack. You have been pounced on my brother and you have cut a deal and made an agreement with Satan".

To be honest with you, I was mad at him for accusing me of cutting a deal with the Devil. Wouldn't you be? So, I prayed about it. And guess what, God told me the same thing Randy had said, only a bit harsher. Thank the Lord that my brother had "Called my bluff" and in a loving way told me what I had done, by spelling it out in plain English. It was then that I realized I had indeed made a deal with the Enemy and had turned control of my life over to him.

The next week, I got back in with my group. I bet you're thinking everything was perfect after I got back in aren't you? Well, it was far from perfect, in fact it was terrifying. The Enemy had me where he wanted me and now I was rebelling against him. So, he immediately stepped up his attacks on me. I went through two weeks of constant assault. I had panic attacks everyday, I was afraid to go anywhere, even to Church! But I sucked it up and went anyway. I couldn't have done it without my brothers praying me through. I stood my ground through that time and the Enemy slowly retreated. I know he is still out there sneaking around the perimeter looking for a weakness and his attacks will come. But today I have the assurance that I can defeat him because of past experience.

Attacks from the realm of Satan come in many forms. The Bible tells us the Enemy is a great deceiver and the language he speaks is lies. Because of this, he loves to turn us against anything that will bring glory to God. For example, have you ever gotten excited about something, maybe a vacation, a possible job opportunity, starting a new ministry, or the like? As time went on, did you ever, in your mind, talk yourself out of it? It's funny to think about, but did you ever hear a voice in your head that downgraded you in some way and told you that you would fail? You are not alone, we all have been attacked in this way.

Lies are the Enemy's first line of attack. If he can condemn you in such a way that it discourages you and keeps you from glorifying God, then he has won. We know from the Bible that there is no condemnation in Christ. This is why it is our duty as Christians to test all spirits. In other words:

> *When you hear a word of condemnation immediately ask yourself if you were to believe the voice would it bring glory to God? If the answer is no, you can be pretty sure that the voice you are hearing is from the Enemy.*

Most of us have been beaten down by attacks for so many years that we accept them as the way life is. This is obvious to me whenever I hear someone use Murphy's Law as an excuse. A big flag goes up every time I hear someone say, "If anything can go wrong, it will". Whenever someone says this to me, it is obvious that they are wandering through life, unaware of the supernatural attacks that are being orchestrated against them. I only wish everyone would stop calling it Murphy's Law, because who is this "Murphy" and what does he have to do with the why and how things happen? Christians need to start calling it what it really is and that is "The Enemy's (Hidden) Standard Operating Procedure".

The Enemy attacks everyone every day but he uses disguise and subtleness in an attempt to fly in just below our spiritual radar. The problem is that most of the time, we see everything through our physical eyes while using our analytical mind to rationalize what we think is going on around us. When we operate this way, we tend to dismiss the supernatural as some type of fantasy that doesn't really exist. Satan may not roar like a lion and announce his unmistakable presence but he's there, prowling around the perimeter of our souls patiently waiting for the perfect opportunity to pounce.

> *When you start to take notice of what's happening around you and begin to identify attacks for what they are, you will have your eyes opened to a whole new world.*

I warn you though! This new world is a scary place to be, even though you are already in it and have been since birth. You have to see it for what it is, a brutal fight for survival with death on all sides of you. To illustrate what the battlefield of this world looks like through spiritual eyes, we have to travel back to 1945. That was the year the most horrific account of survival known to man occurred to an unlikely group of sailors in the South Pacific.

The USS Indianapolis was the flagship of the 5th Fleet and served gloriously throughout the Pacific Theater of operation. Near the end of the war, she had the honor of transporting the atomic bombs that would be dropped on Hiroshima and Nagasaki to their staging point on the island of Tinian in the Pacific. After the bombs were dropped off, the Indianapolis traveled to Guam and then set sail for Okinawa. On July 30, 1945 in rout to Okinawa and unescorted, two explosions rocked her starboard side, causing her to capsize and sink in only twelve minutes.

Since the Indianapolis was on a secret mission, its route was not documented and nobody knew where it was located when it sank. And to make matters worse, it sank so fast that no distress call was given and lifeboats could not be deployed. So all of the sailors not killed by the blasts went into the water to float and await rescue. The big problem with waiting for rescue was that with no record of sailing, the ship was never reported as overdue, and no search party was ever to be sent out.

The survivors were left to float in the open ocean for days hanging on to whatever debris they could latch on to. They were without food, water, and protection of any kind. As if this were not enough, the sailors were simultaneously devoured by sharks. One by one, they watched their friends ripped to shreds and feasted upon. This feeding frenzy continued night and day and every sailor had no idea if they were next. It wasn't until almost a week later that the surviving crew members were spotted by a passing plane, and a rescue was put into action.

In one of my favorite movies ("Jaws"), the plight of the crew of the Indianapolis was made famous by the monologue of the crusty old seaman, Captain Quint. Quint described the terrifying details of the sinking to a naïve young scientist named Hooper (played by Richard Dreyfuss) and the Chief of Police Brody played by Roy Scheider.

Hooper: "You were on the Indianapolis?"

Brody: "What happened?

Quint: "Japanese submarine slammed two torpedoes into her side, Chief. Happened just after midnight. We was coming back from the island of Tinian to Leyte. We'd just delivered the bomb. The Hiroshima bomb. Eleven hundred men went into the water. Vessel went down in 12 minutes. Didn't see the first shark for about a half-hour. Tiger, 13-footer. You know how you know that in the water, Chief? You can tell by looking from the dorsal to the tail. What we didn't know, was that our bomb mission was so secret, no distress signal had been sent. They didn't even list us overdue for a week. Very first light, Chief, sharks come cruisin' by, so we formed ourselves into tight groups. It was sorta' like you see in the calendars, you know the infantry squares in that old calendar over there like the Battle of

Waterloo and the idea was the shark come to the nearest man, that man he starts poundin' and hollerin' and sometimes that shark he'd go away... but sometimes he wouldn't go away. Sometimes that shark looks right at ya'. Right into your eyes. And the thing about a shark is he's got lifeless eyes. Black eyes. Like a doll's eyes. When he comes at ya, he doesn't even seem to be living... 'til he bites ya, and those black eyes roll over white and then... oh then you hear that terrible high-pitched screaming. The ocean turns red, and despite all your poundin' and your hollerin' all those sharks come in and... they rip you to pieces. You know by the end of that first dawn, lost a hundred men. I don't know how many sharks there were, maybe a thousand. I do know how many men, they averaged six an hour. On Thursday morning, the third day Chief, I bumped into a friend of mine, Herbie Robinson from Cleveland. Baseball player. Bosun's mate. I thought he was asleep. I reached over to wake him up. He bobbed up, down in the water in his lifejacket, he was like a kinda top. Upended him into a nearby raft... well, he'd been bitten in half below the waist. At noon on the fifth day, a Lockheed Ventura swung in low and he spotted us, a young pilot, lot younger than Mr. Hooper here, anyway he spotted us and a few hours later a big ol' fat PBY come down and started to pick us up. You know that was the time I was most frightened. Waitin' for my turn. I'll never put on a lifejacket again. So, eleven hundred men went into the water. 316 men came out, the sharks took the rest, June the 29th, 1945. Anyway, we delivered the bomb."

To me, this is the rawest form of terror I can imagine. Floating in the open ocean with a real enemy swimming through your ranks at all times sizing you up and picking off his prey one by one. The horror of the sailors as they watched their friends torn to shreds terrifies me because in their mind they had to be thinking, "Am I next?".

The fate of these sailors floating in the open ocean is an accurate representation of the unseen world around us.

Right now Satan's emissaries are patrolling the sea of life around you searching for a weakness, and waiting to devour you. Although you can't literally see them, they are very real and are really there. I like to think to myself when I am out and about that I see subtle glimpses of a dorsal fin here, and a tail fin there. It reminds me to stay on guard. It also keeps me in-tune with seeing through the eyes of my heart. If this seems too much for you, start out by looking where the enemy is in plain view at all times. You can start by watching the news.

Every night, my wife and I watch the evening news. The news is filled with violence, death, evil, and just when you thought they couldn't possibly top the previous night's debauchery, they do! Usually, the first five minutes are all I need to know that the Enemy is alive and thriving on the Earth. This is especially true when you hear that a three year old was violently abused by her father, a mother has murdered her children, genocide, terrorism, and the list goes on and on. With this display of evil, you can bet your bottom dollar the Enemy has his hand in it.

Another place the Enemy always shows up is in the current event hot topics. Over the last three decades, the topic of abortion has been thrust into the limelight and has set the scene for many violent and deadly clashes. Abortion ruins lives of adults and kills millions of innocent, unborn children each year. You can rest assured that he is right in the middle of abortion because the Bible tells us he is a murderer and it is clear that he hates all of God's children.

What about the family unit? Satan hates families because it is the first institution that God set up when he gave Eve to Adam. And to make matters worse, Satan is infuriated with the fact that marriage ultimately symbolizes Christ and the Church. Remember, anything that brings glory to God, he hates and attacks to destroy, and if he has his way, utterly kill it. If he can't kill something, he will at least seek to divide it. He's doing a pretty good job considering half of all marriages end in divorce. His strategy to divide and conquer is never so evident than in the bonds of marriage.

We've established that the enemy is the sneakiest, craftiest, and most evil being on Earth today. Because he is the most prideful being on Earth, you would logically think that he would want more credit for his work wouldn't you? The opposite is true because he would rather have us believe that he's not really there. I'm sure he licks his chops every time we choose to think he is not a factor in our daily walk. The greatest lie that the Enemy uses to deceive Christians is that he's not here and is not coming against us.

Think about it, have any of you ever seen the Devil? Not the red suit and pitchfork variety, but the real Satan? Sure you have if you know where to look. Like we discussed, everyday you can see spiritual glimpses of the Enemy in the news, at work, anywhere there is suffering, pain, and evil deeds being carried out, you can rest assured that the Devil is there.

But why do we choose not to believe in him? The answer to this question can be found in the teachings of the majority of Churches today. Today's Church has somehow convinced us that because we live in America, we don't have as much spiritual warfare going on. If asked, I would bet that most Christians believe spiritual warfare only happens in underdeveloped countries where black magic and voodoo are as common as Baptists and Pentecostals. Our sophistication has blinded us and caused us to fail to recognize the warfare raging in our own backyard. Obviously we are slowly having our oxygen supply cut off. When this happens we will die a slow and painful death by suffocation like the lion does to the zebra.

If you have gone through life choosing to believe that spiritual warfare is not real, wake up! Also, pick up your Bible and see what it says about spiritual battles. The Bible is a living testament to the epic battle between good and evil. Throughout this perfect work you find the testimony of God and Satan's constant struggle as shown in the following verses:

"We know that we are the children of God and that the whole world is under the control of the evil one." (1 John 5:19)

"Be very careful, then, how you live- not as unwise but as wise making the most of every opportunity, because the days are evil." (Ephesians 5:15,16)

"Skin for skin!" Satan replied. "A man will give all he has for his own life. But stretch out your hand and strike his flesh and bones, and he will surely curse you to your face." (Job 2:4-5)

".....Satan himself masquerades as an angel of light." (II Cor 11:14)

These verses are only the tip of the iceberg when it comes to the relationship between Satan, Man, and God. There are many more examples found in scripture. What I want you, the reader to understand is that Satan is working today the same as he did in the Garden of Eden and in the time of Jesus. Believe me, he's there and waiting to attack you when the time is right.

When I speak of the Enemy attacking, I want to make sure you understand I am including not only him but also his enormous army. If I were to guess, Satan is probably not attacking you personally because I'm sure he has bigger fish to fry. The majority of attacks against Christians are most likely carried out by his well trained and very real army of fallen angels (or demons) and I'm sad to say, they know you all to well. They also have knowledge of exactly which one of your hot buttons to push and when to push them.

Up to this point, I have attempted to show you the obvious signs that the Enemy and his forces are alive and well on planet Earth if you know where to look. Now let's talk about the hidden, more subdued attacks that the Enemy levels against us every day. What I'm referring to here are the attacks to our unseen, private realm that we don't freely talk about let alone allow anyone to see. The Enemy knows how you act in the public eye, and he also knows exactly how you are in private. He also knows exactly how to turn up the heat in your private world with the ultimate goal of driving a wedge in the relationship between you and God.

One of the ways he can enter your private world is to hit you while you are unconscious. This happened to me the other night when I was attacked, of all times, while I was asleep. I awoke in a panic-like state because I dreamed that I was pursuing a girl for sex. I was physically sick in my stomach and felt feverish. By the grace of God, I identified it as an attack and took it to the Him in prayer. As I settled into prayer, I had a voice in my head tell me, "You want her don't you?" I immediately recognized that voice as the Enemy. I prayed and asked Jesus to rescue me from this attack and I commanded the spirits that were assaulting me to flee in the His name and go to judgment at the cross of Calvary. Guess what, after praying it through, the fog lifted and the images, sickness, and voices were gone. This is only one of many incidents that I have lived through in which the Enemy struck me with surgical precision. When the Enemy of our souls pulls the trigger, be assured that he has done his homework before he makes any move.

By now, you're probably thinking, "Man that's pretty creepy stuff. Maybe Donny has some mental issues to work out. You know, all of those voices and stuff". If this is what you are thinking, wake up! You need to see the Enemy for what he is and what methods he employs to attack us. It's high time you stop denying his very real presence and know that you are in daily hand-to-hand combat with him.

The good news for the child of the King is this – I've read the Bible and we win in the end! However, it will get worse before it gets better because the Enemy knows this also. He knows his time is limited and he will stop at nothing to separate you from God. It's up to you to be on guard at all times and identify attacks for what they are; assaults on your heart and your relationship with God. To attempt to separate you from God, the Enemy will try to confuse, divide, tempt, and utterly destroy you. Now that you know to expect constant attacks, be strong and have confidence that you are living a life that pleases God. Remember, the Enemy concentrates his attacks on those that are taking ground for the Kingdom of God. He has little use for the lost because they are already his.

Chapter 2
The Double Agent Stalks

I hate to be the one to tell you this, but there is a traitor among us. In fact, you know him all too well. Believe it or not, this traitor may come across as your number one fan. In fact, he wants nothing but your "self" to come first. He is ruthless, cocky, and arrogant to the point that he wants you to be ahead of God in everything. In this same manner, he hates the purity of God and lives by one rule, "If it feels good, do it!". Children of God, you not only have the outward enemy of Satan and his goons, but you also have a sinister *double agent* inside of you known as the flesh and its goal is to rule your mind.

The flesh is the sinful nature that every human carries with them thanks to Adam and Eve. This sinful nature that we received in the fall of man is driven by a passion for producing evil works. Our sinful flesh can be more destructive and cause more damage than even Satan himself because the flesh is a part of us. It is always with us and is continually emitting evil cravings. Don't feel like you have failed in your Christian walk because you have desires of the flesh. We all do. Me, you, your pastor, even the Pope is not immune to struggles with the flesh.

When we think evil thoughts that are not of God and are lacking in purity, you can bet they are from the flesh. The Apostle Paul wrote two chapters to the Galatians (Chapters 5 and 6) about the flesh in which he urges them to deny the flesh and live by the Spirit.

> "So I say, live by the Spirit, and you will not gratify the desires of the sinful nature. For the sinful nature desires what is contrary to the Spirit, and the Spirit what is contrary to the sinful nature. They are in conflict with each other, so that you do not do what you want." (Gal 5:16-17)

One cannot serve two masters especially when it comes to the Spirit and the flesh. The flesh and the Spirit of God are polar opposites of each other and are constantly warring for control of you. The flesh will ultimately tear apart the Christian's spiritual life if it is not exposed. It is always working against the good things God is doing in your heart and opposes the good fruits of your life. The flesh bears evil fruit as shown in the following verses:

> "The acts of the sinful nature are obvious: sexual immorality, impurity and debauchery;

idolatry and witchcraft; hatred, discord, jealousy, fits of rage, selfish ambition, dissensions, factions and envy; drunkenness, orgies, and the like. I warn you, as I did before, that those who live like this will not inherit the Kingdom of God." (Gal 5:19-21)

Paul pretty much covers everything evil in this passage that humans are capable of doing. Now I'm sure that if you've heard a few sermons and gone to Sunday School long enough, you are no doubt familiar with the aforementioned roll-call of evil. I know I sure was, but I had never really thought about how each of them affects my daily life. I admit thinking, "I've never had an affair on my wife, so I must be living pretty good". How self righteous! Sexual immorality and impurity is only one of the aforementioned items. If you believe like I do that a sin is a sin, then there is no difference between having an affair on your wife and being jealous of your neighbor's new car. It's all sin.

But let's go a little deeper. For instance, has anyone ever cut you off on the highway and caused you to fly into a fit of rage, cursing and gesturing? Maybe you didn't go to that extreme, maybe you internalized it and held back hoping one day you would get your revenge (hatred). What about the idols in your life? You know, the stuff that you really love such as your boat, car, dog, etc. Think about it this way, anything that takes precedent over God is an idol. I have some friends that are so involved in their children's pursuits that they have little time for their own spiritual relationship with God. Has it ever crossed your mind that your kids can be idols, no different than a golden calf from the Old Testament that is worshiped instead of God? It's scary to think about what the real love of our lives are and compare them with what God desires. And what about adultery? Didn't Jesus say that if you even look upon a woman in lust you have committed adultery in your mind? You guessed it, we are all sinners but we can be forgiven.

As you can see, we are all guilty of committing sins mentioned in this roll call of evil. The scary thing is that the flesh and the Enemy have made each one of us feel comfortable in our day to day sin. By working in tandem and feeding each others fires, they have helped our minds to subdue the realization of sins that we are committing. Not only does the battle rage around you, it rages in your mind where the flesh and the Enemy have but one agenda: To undermine God's good and perfect will for your life by convincing you to put things ahead of Him, telling you how good you're doing, and utterly killing you after they have distanced you from God.

But why would the flesh, our own flesh, want to kill us? That may sound a bit absurd and you may have even conjured up images of suicide, but let's look at what Paul wrote to the Romans:

> "For when we were controlled by the sinful nature, the sinful passions aroused by the law were at work in our bodies, so that we bore fruit for death." (Rom 7:5)

44

Paul tells us in black and white that before we were Christians, we did not live for God. Our lives were self-led (by our flesh) and sin ridden. Since the Bible also tells us that the wages of sin is death, you can see that living by the flesh leads **only** to death. Now I'm not saying that a Christian is never going to sin, believe me, it is inevitable. You will sin, but by being on guard and listening to God's leading you will definitely do a better job of identifying sin before it ensnares you. We will never be sinless but we can sin less when we walk with the Spirit as our guide.

If you'll remember in the previous chapter I talked about how the Enemy and his army's **only** goal is to steal, kill, and destroy (John 10:10). It's no wonder that the flesh and the Enemy are like old hunting buddies, they both have us in their cross-hairs! The good news is that there is an "Achilles heal" of the flesh and it can be exploited by the Spirit of God. But how do we use the Holy Spirit to strike at this weakness? We start by talking to the Holy Spirit and building a dependency upon Him. He has already taken up residence in your heart the day you were converted so you have Him all the time. Praying to the Holy Spirit that he will fill you, expose your fleshly desires, and rid them from your life by purifying you are the easy part. It gets a little difficult when it comes to listening to His direction and even harder to do exactly what he tells you without question. But I'm not talking about trusting in the Spirits guidance from time to time. I'm talking about a life-long commitment to a daily walk with Him where you must ask Him which way to go and let Him direct not one, but all of your paths. When we live by the Holy Spirit's guidance and allow Him to dominate our lives, we cannot help but bear His fruits instead of those of the flesh. .

But why is it so hard to do what God tells us? You know, he did create the universe and everything in it, it looks like we would trust him automatically. But could it be due to the fact that we are untrusting beings because of our sinful nature and that whole fall of man thing? That's part of it I'm sure, but what it all boils down to is that all men are by nature, "Control Freaks". We like to think we are in control of our lives at all times. It is not until we come to the realization that God is the only one that is really in control and we put all (and I mean all) of our trust in him, can we live our life to bring glory to him.

Don't think that I am any better than you in this battle, because I struggle with this control issue everyday. It seems like some days you take a giant leap forward spiritually only to be shoved back the next day. But that's ok, at least you are in the battle! When we fix our eyes on God and at least try to turn our lives over to Him, He blesses and you grow in His wisdom. Like most of you, I hope to one day live a life that is totally dependent upon the Spirit's guidance when I will be able to easily recognize the flesh and have strength to refuse to obey its desires.

Because He is such an awesome God, He gave us another solution to overcome the flesh. This happens when we come to the realization that the fleshly power of sin was nullified by the sacrifice of our Savior Jesus Christ. That is what he died for, to free us from not only the sin of this world but also from the sin of ourselves. The Bible tells us:

"I have been crucified with Christ and I no longer live, but Christ lives in me. The life I live in the body, I live by faith in the Son of God, who loved me and gave himself for me." (Gal 2:20)

and

"Those who belong to Christ Jesus have crucified the sinful nature with its passions and desires." (Gal 5:24)

Paul tells us that when we accept Christ, the flesh is put to death and we become a new creation. We are reborn as a new person by the same power that raised Christ from the dead and a new heart is created within us. What an awesome work of God! But the battle has really just been intensified. Because we are a new creation, the flesh wants back in. He has been kicked out of his nice comfy home and sent packing. How would you like it if you were kicked out of your house and told your weren't welcome, even though you have an original claim to it? I know I would fight to keep what was mine and do whatever it took to reclaim my ground. The flesh is no different. It will fight back by first going after your mind.

The human mind is like a piece of prime real estate that the flesh seeks to occupy and set up shop. In fact, he wants to build a factory in your mind that pumps out evil desires 24/7. *Your mind is the most hotly contest piece of ground that is fought for in Christian warfare.* The flesh seeks to claim it and the Enemy wants to dominate it and direct you. But how do we fight this battle? We must start by asking ourselves the question, "What is my mind occupied with?" When you are walking in the flesh, your mind is always thinking about pleasing the desires of your sinful nature. Your mind is only thinking "Me, Me, Me". The good news is this: that is not the way God created you. God designed you to walk with him and let him steer the direction of your life. The problem is, there is too much "*self- stuff*" jamming up our lives today.

I was at a local bookstore a while back and I happened upon the non-Christian "Self-Help Section". It was a massive area of book shelves that were jammed full of books about how you can make yourself smarter, improve your memory, lose weight, beat Vegas, lower stress, get rich, etc. Just about any topic you can imagine has a book that claims to have it all figured out. The underlying theme of all these books is this: You can do anything by simply harnessing the power of your mind. At first I thought it was silly but then I realized how popular these books really are. As a Christian, this scared me because that section of the store had about ten people in it that were obviously searching for what they thought they needed. My heart told me that they are missing it altogether.

When I got home that evening, I started thinking about my Christian walk and how I can't make it without God's help. I thought to myself, "How did I make it all of those years without him?". The answer was pretty clear, I didn't. It wasn't until I surrendered my life to him, and started living from my heart that I really began to live. Looking back on the many years I spent without God, it saddens me to think that in all of that time I was going at life alone and leaning on my own intellect to carry me through. Boy is that scary. It's only by his grace that I am even here today.

Obviously, the writers of Self-Help books are living life like I did, before I placed my trust in God and accepted his leadership. I'm sure these folks mean well and are honestly trying to help people instead of just trying to make a quick buck. But when you think about their writings from the Christian point of view it's obvious they have "missed the boat" spiritually speaking. Think about it, all of these works are dependant on YOU helping YOURSELF and God is completely left out of the equation. In other words, the key to the success of self help is by your flesh helping your flesh. As my Grandma would say "That's like putting a rooster in a hen house!"

Our self ability is limited by the gray matter we carry around in our heads. Granted, the human mind is the most complex and powerful computer ever built. But who built it? And once again, self is flesh and flesh is the enemy of the spiritual. Being a child of God means we have died to self and have "Put off the old man" when we were converted. Every Christian has within their hearts the all knowing, all powerful, and all helping God of the universe in the form of His Holy Spirit. It is not until we give up trying to logically examine everything and trust in him that we can truly run in paths of his commands.

The Apostle Paul wrote to the Christians living in Rome about not living in the flesh. Paul labels the flesh as the sinful nature that is inherent to all humans when he wrote:

> "Therefore, brothers, we have an obligation-but it is not to the sinful nature, to live according to it. For if you live according to the sinful nature, you will die; but if by the Spirit you put to death the misdeeds of the body, you will live, because those who are led by the Spirit of God are sons of God." (Romans 8:12-14)

He's pretty straightforward about the fact that if you live by the fleshy sinful nature, you will die and be separated from God. What he also does here is tell them what to do to fix it. In order to kill the misdeeds of the body (the flesh) we must walk with the Holy Spirit, listening to his guidance instead of our own.

When you walk in the Spirit, you want to please Christ. Since the flesh wants what is the opposite of the Spirit's desire, there is a constant struggle between the two. No one is immune to this battle, not even the Apostle Paul! He wrote:

> "I know that nothing good lives in me, that is, in my sinful nature. For I have the desire to do what is good, but I cannot carry

it out. For what I do is not the good I want
to do; no, the evil I do not want to do-this
I keep on doing. Now if I do what I do not
want to do, it is no longer I who do it, but it
is sin living in me that does it. So I find this
law at work: When I want to do good, evil is
right there with me. For in my inner being I
delight in God's law; but I see another law
at work in the members of my body, waging
war against the law of my mind and making
me a prisoner of the law of sin at work within
my members." (Romans 7:18-23)

This is the battle of the mind from which you can
never relax. The moment you let down your guard,
the flesh and the Enemy are ready to strike with all
kinds of sinful ideas in an attempt to take back what
was stolen from them.

You may be asking, "How do I differentiate
between the attacks of the Enemy and the desires of
the flesh?" The answer is, there is no easy way to tell.
You have to use the goodness of your heart and the
counsel of the Holy Spirit to help you identify your
assailant. The flesh and Satan are very closely related
and sometimes hard to differentiate. Because Satan
rules the evilness of this world and the flesh is inher-
ently evil, it is safe to say that Satan is the master
of the flesh. However, we've already established that
Satan is a being unto himself that conducts warfare
against us. We have to assume that one of the most
powerful weapons that Satan wields against us is our
own flesh. So in other words, Satan has an insider or

a double agent that is with you at all times trying to trip you up.

One of the best examples of the flesh that I have seen is in the lust of the eyes. How many times have you been driving along and noticed a woman jogging and stolen a quick glance? Or better yet, once you have passed her have you ever checked her out again in your rearview mirror? In that short period of time, you evaluated her, thought about what it would be like, and when you looked for a second time, you took her. That is one of the rawest forms of fleshly desires in a man known as lust. What we fail to realize is that what we are doing is sin. Thus enters the Enemy that whispers a lie to the effect of, "It's ok to look, as long as you don't touch." Jesus told us that if we even so much as look upon a woman in lust, we have already committed adultery in our hearts. So who do you believe? I hope you picked Jesus.

This is just one of many examples of how the flesh will cause us to fail and become separated from God. The Enemy's attack in this instance is just the icing on the cake. There are countless other examples that do not involve members of the opposite sex. One that I see all too often is when we just have to own the newest greatest thing that you can show off in front of everyone. It may be a car, truck, boat, watch, or any number of objects that will ultimately break down, lose their value, and rust away. Jesus made this clear in one of my favorite passages when he spelled it out by saying:

"Do not store up for yourselves treasures on earth, where moth and rust destroy, and where thieves break in and steal. But store up for yourselves treasures in heaven, where moth and rust do not destroy, and where thieves do not break in and steal. For where your treasure is, there your heart will be also." (Matt 6:19-21)

In a nutshell, we all have voids in our life. The problem is that our flesh will always try to fill them with things of this world and not of God. We need to be ever diligent in detecting this tendency and make every effort we can to fill the voids with God. He's got an endless supply to give us if only we ask.

Some of you are probably saying, "I give up! I can never live like a true Christian because my flesh always gets me." Yep! You're right and I feel like that sometimes too. The good news is that we have what I like to call a get out of jail free card that we can use and it is called *grace*. Grace is God's boundless love for us that he gives without end even though we do not deserve it. It's a hard thing to explain because we cannot think like God and comprehend the love he has for us. Look at it this way, He sent his only son and let Him be killed because of grace! It is beyond me to understand it and the best way I can say it is the grace of God really is amazing.

However, grace is not to be misused or abused. We can't go through life with the attitude, "Well I'm about to screw up again, I'll have to ask for forgiveness later". That doesn't work because what we are really doing is slapping God in the face and taking Him for granted. God wants our genuine selves and he wants to forgive us but it takes devotion on our part for him to pour out his blessings on our lives. In order to tap into God's grace and receive the blessing, it also takes a daily commitment from us. We must totally surrender ourselves to him daily as a living sacrifice and an offering to be used by him.

This Amazing Grace is a primary component of God's forgiveness of us. He gives it without regard and he also gives us free will to accept or reject it. And even if we reject it, it's still there for the taking. God's desire for us is to do His will and not the world's. John tells us:

> "Do not love the world or anything in the world. If anyone loves the world, the love of the Father is not in him. For everything in the world-the cravings of sinful man, the lust of his eyes and the boasting of what he has and does-comes not from the Father but from the world. The world and its desires pass away, but the man who does the will of God lives forever." (I John 2:15-17)

Plain, simple, and straight forward, God loves you and wants all of you for His purposes. He has a job description that only you fit, and best of all He designed you for it! He also wants you with Him for eternity and the only thing separating you from Him is the fleshly desires of this world. No one ever said it was going to be easy following Christ, but it is worth it.

Chapter 3
Male Pattern Blindness

Have you been "Chasing the American Dream"? Have you bought in to the lie that "He who dies with the most toys wins"? I will be the first one to admit that this was me just a few years ago. I spent a lot of time and effort earning money so I could buy whatever struck my fancy. That is the American Dream isn't it? The only problem is that when I became a Christian, I had a hard time trying to serve the two masters in my life at that time which were God and money. I know I am not alone in this struggle, because all men are goal oriented and look at their careers as a great game that they must win. But do we really win?

When we take our eyes off of God and focus in on the things of this world such as careers and money, we have been afflicted with what I like to call **male pattern blindness** or **MPB** for short. MPB strikes all men at some time in their life. It is a chronic condition of the heart brought on by the fleshly desires of this world. Over time, MPB will weaken your relationship with God and ultimately isolate you from him, denying you of all the blessings He so desires to give you. Some of the symptoms of MPB include:

- Worried about physical appearance all the time.
- Always checking stocks, 401K, or other investments.
- Envy the guy driving the newest SUV on the market.
- Would kill for a Rolex.
- Afraid to ask for help from anyone.
- Will never admit he is getting older.
- Needs more stuff to take up more space.
- Is never wrong about anything.

MPB can only be cured by a close relationship with THE Great Physician. It can be a painful and lengthy treatment program because you must **let** Him transform you. But fear not, He can cure anything, and your insurance premium won't even go up!

The ball is in your court and only you can start the process of healing. The process begins when the man seeks out and grabs a hold of his only savior Jesus Christ. Of course, you must first recognize that you are blind and you must have the desire to change. Then you must ask for and let God heal your heart and mind. God must be aloud to heal the man's heart by first re-prioritizing his life. This starts with the eyes. The Apostle Paul wrote to the Hebrews a verse that sums this up.

"Let us fix our **eyes** on Jesus, the author and perfecter of our faith…" (Hebrews 12:2)

By fixing our eyes on Jesus and not things of this world we can get started with the healing process. Next, we must refocus the heart and mind as Paul also wrote:

"Since then, you have been raised with Christ, set your **hearts** on things above, where Christ is seated at the right hand of God. Set your **minds** on things above, not on earthly things." (Col 3:1-2)

Only when our eyes, hearts, and minds are focused on heavenly things can we get ourselves on the right track to overcoming MPB.

After we learn to refocus our body parts, it will be easier to reorder the pursuit of things in this world. When we chase after the things of this world trying to get ahead of the pack, we are only interested in "Castle Building". The Pastor of my Church once told me that men in general are all about "Castle Building". In other words, we want money, houses, cars, and all the other "stuff" of this world. Men most often view these things as a way to keep score with others in the game of life. Unlike a football game with a scoreboard in full view, our life doesn't have a running tally of how we measure up with other guys around us. Men chase after the things of this world in an attempt to collect as much stuff in as little time as possible. This is exactly the opposite of what God wants for our lives. God does not care about what kind of car you drive or how many square feet your home takes up. God wants "Kingdom Builders" not "Castle Builders".

One of the ways I used to keep score was by looking at a man's watch. I used to be so impressed by watches that I would size a man up simply by looking at the hardware he carried on his wrist. In my mind, I had devised a score sheet that told me if he had on a rubber watch, I figured he worked out a lot and could probably kick my butt. If he wore a Rolex, he could most likely buy and sell me. But if the poor guy had on a watch from Wal-Mart forget it, I was way above him. What a lie I believed from the Enemy that I had unconsciously bought into. Once I identified this ugly part of my life and after much prayer and healing, I soon realized that God doesn't wear a watch.

Ask a woman what she thinks is wrong with men today and you will get any number of responses. You will hear just about every bad thing imaginable such as lazy, disengaged, and cowardly. As mentioned earlier, we bear the image of God and He is none of those qualities. So what has gone wrong with the men of today?

To explore this problem, I started doing my homework on what us "guys" are worrying the most about in life. During my research, I ran into a friend of mine that told me he knew for certain Ben Franklin was right when he said the only two things you can count on are death and taxes. In a way he is right, but my friend has obviously come down with a case of MPB and needs some urgent care and medical attention. God did not create us to live our lives in a boring and dismal state looking at each day as a "To Do" list that must be finished before we go to sleep, only to get up and do it all over again. God created us to glorify him and worship him. It's pretty obvious that the Enemy and his good buddy flesh have done a fine job misleading men over the years.

To go a little deeper, I asked some honest men the same question that I had asked the women. When I say "honest men" I am talking about straight shooters that will tell you what's on their heart and not feel weak doing it. In other words, these guys have overcome MPB. The overwhelming answer that I heard from them was that all men have too much on their plate these days. That leads me to the first characteristic of today's male: **Busy.**

When you think about it men, you are statistically speaking, the bread winner of the family. We've all heard the slogan "a dollar doesn't go as far as it used too", never is that more true than today. This leaves men in a tight spot trying to provide for their families. Also, the safety and security of your loved ones has fallen into your lap and it is probably the hardest, most worrisome job you will ever have. In today's world there is only one way to provide all of these things and that way is to stay busy.

More is expected of men today than at any other time in history and it is slowly killing them. In fact, busyness is a cancer on the man of today that if left untreated will lead to death, distant from God. But why are we so busy? Let's dig in and look at the way we are brought up and taught to be men.

From the time we can walk, we are told that if you keep your nose to the grindstone, you will succeed. The only problem with this logic is that when your nose is to the grindstone, it's hard to see what's going on around you. Also, if you're not careful, the grindstone can cut your nose off your face. There needs to be a balance between your spiritual walk, work, and family. This turns men into jugglers.

I have always been fascinated by juggling and it's probably because I stink at it. I used to be able to juggle two golf balls in one hand for about ten seconds but that's as good as I ever got. What amazes me about juggling is the knowledge that the juggler has about the objects he is continually throwing up in the air. The juggler knows the exact amount of force (or touch) to put on each item as he quickly catches and tosses it.

Men are basically jugglers of the things of life. Most times, I have about twelve different items up in the air all at once. The bad thing is they don't all weigh or feel the same. To nail down how busy I am, I made a list of everything I do throughout a given week. What I found was that I juggled being a coach, a personnel manager, an environmental coordinator, a father, a husband, a safety director, a Church member, a Sunday School Teacher, a security officer, an insurance specialist, a landscape architect (weed puller), a baby sitter, a mechanic, and a referee.

All of these are totally different and each requires its own specific touch. I liken it to juggling a steak knife, a bowling ball, a chainsaw, and a fuzzy pillow all at once. Throw one up in the air too hard or not fast enough, your timing gets off and they all come tumbling down right on top of your head.

Sir Isaac Newton proved that what goes up must come down, it's inevitable. So I'll ask you this question today: What are you juggling that is causing you the most stress? Is it worth it to God and your family to lay it down? Busyness for monetary gain never got anyone into heaven or gained them an extra day on earth. Take my advice, "He who dies with the most toys, still dies".

With that said, I want you to take a step back and think about what you just read and reflect upon your own private world. How busy are you? Is it distracting to you? Busyness is the cornerstone of the Enemy's attacks. When we are busy, we have less time to focus on the will of God for our lives. Remember that God created you for his pleasure and he longs for a deep relationship with you. That is why you were created, not to become the greatest salesman, doctor, teacher, etc. on the planet, but to please God.

When we're overly busy, we also have less time to devote to relationships in our own family. If we don't have time for our own family, you can forget about having meaningful relationships with anyone outside of your home. The bottom line is that busyness causes separation not only from God but from your family, friends, and other relationships that are crucial to your Christian walk.

When I started writing this book, I set out to show men how to build a culture of warriors around them. We'll get into that later but right now I want to talk about why you need brothers that will fight with you and do battle for you. First and foremost we've got God's word on it that he wants it that way! Ecclesiastes 4:9-12 tells us:

"Two are better than one, because they have a good return for their work: If one falls down, his friend can help him up. But pity the man who falls and has no one to help him up!" (Ecclesiastes 4:9-10)

Pity the man who falls and has no one to help him up, God is obviously serious about people walking with each other and most of all helping and fighting for each other. He goes on to tell us:

"Also, if two lie down together they will keep warm. But how can one keep warm alone?" (Ecclesiastes 4:11)

This verse is a key point to this book: You must have other men around you to keep you warm and strengthen you in your walk with God. You were not designed to go it alone. Most of all you need other men around you as a source to draw strength from. He goes on:

"Though one may be overpowered, two
can defend themselves. A cord of three strands
is not quickly broken." (Ecclesiastes 4:12)

A few years ago, the new wave in Christianity
drew from these verses to convince many of us to
get a friend that would be known as an accountability partner. Your accountability partner would
be someone whom you could tell all of your weaknesses too and confide in them just how many times
you slipped up each week. Who ever thought this up?
Talk about lack of action! It doesn't take a rocket
scientist to figure out that these verses aren't telling
us to find an accountability partner to confess too.
These verses tell us that we need soldiers on the
ground with us, slugging it out with the enemy in
daily, hand-to-hand combat.

As you can see, we've got God's word that he
desires us to have deep and meaningful relationships with others. To piggyback these Old Testament
verses, in the New Testament, Paul told the Romans
it was vital to their survival when he wrote:

"Be devoted to one another in brotherly
love. Honor one another above yourselves"
(Rom 12:10)

With that said, let's move on to the next characteristic of today's male: He is **Isolated**. The average
Church man of today has no close friends, only
acquaintances. He may know the first name of a few
guys, if he's lucky. Otherwise he'll fake it the best he

can. He may see them on Sundays and Wednesdays and have a conversation as follows:

"Hey Stan! How's it going?", "Great Dave, Just Great! God's been blessing me this week. God is so good!", "He sure is Stan, all the time God is good", "I'll be praying for you!", "And I'll be praying for you too brother!"

And that's it, how fake! Stan and Dave are obviously trying not to talk to each other aren't they? But, I've had this conversation and I'm sure you have at some time in your life. Did you ever think how superficial this is? Did you ever think how you are hiding behind your true heart? Do you really think that deep down Stan and Dave really care about how each one is doing? And better yet, will either one of them pray for each other at all this week? I'd doubt it. I'm sure that Stan and Dave were happy to be out of the conversation as soon as they left each other's site.

As men, we often have these types of conversations that consist of mainly questions with no answers. There's no depth, it's all on the surface. Stan and Dave never develop a deep relationship because like most men, they equate distance with safety and security. But why? I don't think you will be too surprised to find that the Enemy's has a hand in it.

I used to be Stan and/or Dave. I went through many superficial relationships in my life for many years. Before I became involved in men's ministry, I could count on one hand all of the other males I have ever had a deep relationship with. There was Chris, my best friend growing up, and Troy, my bunkmate in Bootcamp. That was it! Two people in the whole world that I ever poured myself into and really got to know on a deep, intimate level. The enemy had me where he wanted me, isolated and cut off from the pack. I was a loner that he could have his way with. It wasn't until I surrounded myself with other Christian warriors that I had any meaningful relationships with anyone other than my wife.

One of the contributing factors to isolation in the Church is due to the fact that we have bought into the Enemy's lie that Christians have to be perfect, and even worse, are not aloud to have problems, or at least not talk about them. Get real! We all have problems and trials in this world. The picture we paint is simply this: We all live a lie and portray everything is just great up in our ivory towers, while in reality our towers are decaying from the inside out.

One of the problems with today's Christianity is that the foundation of our ivory towers is made out of bricks formed from years of playing Church. Most people, whether they realize it or not, have been taught by the Church to portray this false image. So, when we see our Church family members on Sundays and Wednesdays, all is well and life is grand! There is a slogan that was very popular years ago but has obviously long since been forgotten:

"Christians aren't perfect, just forgiven"

We have been duped by the Enemy into believing that Christians have to be perfect. I hope I am not the first to tell you that there was only one person that ever walked the earth and He was perfect.

Another way men isolate themselves is by hiding out in the different ministries of the Church as helpers. A while back, one of my closest brothers approached a man that's been going through an extremely difficult time in his life. His marriage was collapsing around him and he was thinking of throwing in the towel. My warrior brother cornered him in the Church lobby and asked him to attend one of our times of prayer, hoping if anything to give this man a show of support from the other men that would fight for him. The man in question told him he couldn't come because he had to help out with a kids group. My brother felt this man's need for help and asked him, "Who can take your place? You need to be with us". The man that's whole world was falling apart around him simply said, "No one.".

I've had similar situations when asking men to come to our men's group and have been turned down because of other ministry commitments. Now, all ministry groups need help, and many are under-staffed, but is there no one out there that can fill in for you? Is there any rest for the weary? Or, are you hiding out?

I'm starting to come to the realization that men like to hide out in other ministries of the Church. Think about it, it's safe there! You don't have to share anything intimate nor do you have to be vulnerable when you are just helping out. Don't get me wrong, I know that everyone is called to their area of ministry where their gifts can be used. But I also know in my heart that everyone needs to be fed, sharpened, and fought for

Men, if you are guilty of hiding out, it's time to stop it and get real. You need your brothers! It's time for men to come together and join each other in this battle we were born into. Even the Lone Ranger had Tonto and we already have God's word that there is strength in numbers. But what about when no one is around and I need help? That is when you can use your brothers the most. It is no secret that the Enemy loves to come at us when we are alone and when nobody is looking, except God of course. I thank God that we live in the information age and that I can get in touch with one of my brothers with the click of a mouse or the touch of a phone. Let's face it guys, with the amount of communication devices out there, you should be able to get in touch with any person at any time, in any weather.

Networks of brothers are crucial to your survival in this world. God intended you to be a hero, not on your own merits, but with the help of other men. The Bible is full of examples of this. Where would David have been without Jonathan, Paul without Barnabus, Moses without Aaron, or Joshua without Caleb? The bottom line is, God made you a man because he has a specific job that only you can do to fulfill his purpose for your life. It takes the strength of other brothers (as shown here) to help bring out this purpose.

The third characteristic of today's male is **Pride**. Every Sunday morning, men all over the world are using pride to get their "game face" on. Usually it is in the parking lot of the Church just before they set foot out of their vehicle. It doesn't matter that he has been yelling at the kids all the way there, when his foot hits the parking lot, he is in essence charging out of the tunnel and onto the playing field. Most men don't realize how damaging this is to them. By living a lie and playing it up for everyone to see, feelings are being suppressed in the deep heart and left there like eggs waiting to hatch. When these feelings finally break out of their little shells, they eat their way out of the man's heart, and eventually show up in violent outbursts.

How many times has it been preached to us from the pulpit that you have to lay down your pride? I'm sure you've heard it umpteen times also. But let me ask you this, have you completely surrendered to pride? I'm the first one to say I haven't. A spirit of pride rears its ugly head often in the life of this man and it all goes back to the way I was raised.

I was brought up to be independent and not rely on anyone else. This turned me into a know-it-all that thought he had all the answers and could never lower himself to ask for help. Oh what opportunities to educate myself that I missed out on because I was afraid to ask questions thinking it would make me look stupid. I know I'm not alone in this because most men would rather suffer in silence then ask another man a question, afraid they may reveal a weakness. Be honest with yourself guys, what does it take for you to stop and ask for directions when you are lost in a new city?

Pride bulldozes through our daily life and alienates us from other men. Have you ever wondered why? If you said the Enemy, you are on the right track. Satan is the author and perfecter (if you can say such a thing) of pride. He is pride! His favorite way to use it is by making men afraid to lean on each other for support. But why you may ask? Think about it, men praying for, walking with, and supporting each other for the Kingdom of God terrifies him. He wants you to be isolated because although you may not know how powerful a group of praying men can be to his schemes, he sure does and he shutters at the thought of it

The Bible is pretty straight forward when it comes to how God feels on this issue for it is written:

"The Lord tears down the proud mans house...." (Proverbs 15:25)

And the scariest one of all to me is,

"Pride goes before destruction, a haughty spirit before a fall"
(Proverbs 16:18)

Wow! Get the point? God hates pride and seeks to destroy it. It makes sense when you realize that Satan is a manifestation of pride. Pride is the ultimate antichrist and it is killing our men.

So, if you find yourself riding the pride bus today, don't wait for the next bus stop to get off. Jump out the window and let your brothers catch you. You may be banged up a little from the fall, but that beats riding with the Enemy of your soul in the driver's seat. If you do stay on, you will ride for a while and probably see some nice scenery along the way but sooner or later, the ride will end when you plunge over the cliff and crash onto the rocks below.

Because the Enemy hunts like a lion and seeks only to steal, kill, and destroy you, you need some help along the pathway of life. If you are not running with the herd, you can rest assured that you are about to be pounced upon and suffocated. But, you don't have to be afraid because you already possess all of the raw materials you need. God designed you to be a warrior!

Chapter 4
The Warrior Soul

When I was in the Army, one of my commanders often spoke of how all soldiers possessed a warrior soul. He elaborated on this one day and told the entire Company that the warrior soul is what drives the soldier on. It is his inner strength and what makes him brave enough to charge up a hill in the thick of battle and take out a machine gun nest. In other words he was saying we all had a warrior's heart for victory not defeat. To this day, I don't know where this particular officer was in his spiritual life but I assume he had some relationship with God because he was obviously in touch with his deep heart.

With that said, let's explore this warrior soul principle a little deeper. When I refer to the Warrior Soul, please do not confuse it with the soul God created within each one of us. What I am talking about is best explained in II Timothy 2:7 when the Apostle Paul told his understudy Timothy:

"For God did not give us a spirit of timidity, but a spirit of power, of love and of self discipline." (II Tim 2:7)

Paul was telling Timothy that God had already done a great work in him that he probably hadn't yet realized. Paul points out that God gave each one of us a spirit of boldness or as I like to translate it, "God gave you GUTS". This is an ideal picture of the warrior soul that all men possess. Many men discount this fact and some even believe it is not within them. I'm here to tell you that it is within you and was written on your heart when God created you.

When God created man, he created us in his image and that image is a warrior. Have you ever thought of God in that way before? Most of us are lead to believe that God is some gray haired majestic old man sitting on a throne surrounded by angels singing "Holy, Holy, Holy". Well, that is somewhat true, but God is much more than that. The Bible is filled with examples where God is portrayed as a mighty warrior. If there is any doubt in your mind about God's warrior nature, turn to Exodus and read about what he did to Pharaoh's Army. But that is just one example. The Scriptures are full of great battles fought by men with God on their side. We are shown over and over how war is a part of God's nature.

Have you ever taken time to think about how our physical design (also God's image) is suited for battle? First of all, God set within us a cunning mind with the ability to strategize, symbolize, and calculate. This mind allows us to size up our competition and evaluate weaknesses. The mind also helps us compare an enemy's strengths with our own weaknesses so that we can develop a plan of attack that will utilize our strengths and keep from exposing our vulnerabilities. God also gave us the ability to coordinate with others through a complicated system of verbalizing our thoughts known as communication. With all of these traits in our arsenal, it is obvious that our mind is well suited for the battlefield

In addition to a cunning mind, God designed our arms, legs, hands, and feet to be strong, swift, and nimble. In fact, every part of our body was precisely designed to perform well in battle. Even the fat we carry on our bellies is strategic! It not only gives us insulation and extra protection, it gives us an energy source to tap into when needed. Let's face it, the human body is a marvel of creation and has no equal on this planet. When compared with stronger animals, what we may lack in physical strength, is more than made up in mental capacity.

The most important part of our entire makeup is that God set within us is a heart. Not the part that is pumping blood within your chest (it is a marvel unto itself). What I am talking about is the center of yourself, your soul. God created in each of us a heart that is the center of our emotions and is the direct pipeline to him. Non-Christians and even some Christians all too often live from their minds, leaving out God, and trusting in their own thoughts and selfish desires.

Living from your heart means you are taking your direction from the Holy Spirit's leading and listening to the voice of God. I went against the still small voice a while back and it cost me dearly.

After having lunch with my wife at her school, I looked at my watch and realized I had to get back to work. I hopped in my Jeep and headed toward the office. I had traveled about two blocks when I heard, "Why don't you take the back way to work?". After calculating the distance in my mind and the time it takes to travel the back way verses the interstate, I told myself, "Nah, the Interstate is quicker". So I proceeded down the road toward the Interstate.

That's when it happened. I was cruising along singing to myself when a car shot out in front of me. I locked up the brakes and started sliding. The last thing I remember seeing was a young lady looking at me from her driver's seat with her mouth open. We hit with a hard thump and sounds of breaking glass and twisting metal. I immediately grabbed my phone and called 911. I saw the girl moving around frantically in the car so I told 911 I didn't think we needed an ambulance. Then the girl got out of her car and I saw the blood on her forehead. And to make it even worse, I watched her remove a 2 year old from the back seat. Frantically, I called 911 back and said, "Send an ambulance now!" I ran to the girl asked if she and the baby were ok. She said she thought she was but was scared. I took the baby from her and helped calm her down. In a few moments, the Sheriff, two Fire Departments, and an Ambulance showed up.

Long story short, all parties were alright, nothing broken except our vehicles. The next morning in my prayer time (in the shower) I thanked God for watching over and protecting us and I also thanked him for changing me from the way I was before knowing him. I really hate to think how I would have reacted to this same incident ten years ago before I knew Jesus. And last but not least I apologized to God for ignoring that still small voice. Believe me, if you fail to listen to him, get ready to have the devil shaken out of you!

Before I go any further, I want you to understand that I am not some super-tuned in to God, higher spiritual plane, religious expert. I'm just a Christian in a relationship with Him trying desperately to listen to his leading. I'm not the only person he is speaking to, he is always speaking to you too hoping you will hear His voice and not discount it as one of your own random thoughts. For instance, have you ever had a gut instinct or a feeling about something that tugged at you so hard you couldn't ignore it? Did you ever think it could be God? I've never heard him thunder the way he did to Moses, but I have sensed him in my heart through subtle tuggings. When we see with the spiritual eyes of our heart and hear with the spiritual ears of our heart, then we can hear him, and most of all obey his words.

You're probably saying, "I've heard of and even sang a few songs about opening the eyes of my heart, but the ears of my heart?". I thought it sounded funny too when I first wrote it in my blog, but lets go deeper into the heart and what it signifies. In the 26th chapter of Exodus, there is a detailed description of the Holiest Place in the Jewish Temple. Under the Old Covenant, the Spirit of God resided in the Holiest Place and only the High Priest could enter once a year, on the Yom Kippur, to sprinkle the blood of a sacrificed animal upon the Ark of the Covenant and the Mercy Seat (the lid) which sat on top of the Ark.

When Jesus came, he brought the new covenant (by His perfect blood sacrifice) and replaced these Jewish practices. Also, He made it so that everyone that believes in him is transformed and is given a pure heart. This pure heart becomes the believer's personal Holiest Place where the Spirit of God resides. It's obvious that our heart is pure and good because God is holy and cannot reside in an unholy place. Think about it, your body is the temple and your heart is the Holiest Place, the Holy of Holies where the Spirit lives.

With that said, because the Spirit lives within us, he is with us always, counseling us and directing our paths. Oswald Chambers said that thinking too much with our brains (over-analysis) can ruin our communion with God when he said "the common sense life can be the enemy of the supernatural life". With that said, when we walk with God by living from our hearts, only then will we better hear him with spiritual ears.

Since our whole being was created in the likeness of a warrior, we can rest assured that He has set a warrior soul within each one of us. An easy way to verify this is to look at the differences between little boys and girls. Being married to an educator provides me with a unique look into how boys and girls differ. I love to visit her school (even days that I have vehicle accidents) because there is always something going on that demonstrates the wild nature of God manifest in young boys.

Many times, after hearing a story of what one boy did to another, I've burst out laughing in celebration of the heart of God. My celebration time is normally cut short when I hear the famous words, "It's not funny!". But, it is a funny thing to me that the majority of the aggressive behavior problems are at the hand of boys. For example, if someone slammed someone else's head in a locker, broke a window, got in a fight, or jumped off a ten foot wall behind the school, you can bet it was a boy. For years, Psychologists have tried their best to diagnose boys with all different kinds of mental defects such as Attention Deficit Disorder (ADD), Hyperactivity Disorder (HD), or a combination of both (ADHD). I hate to break it to you Doc, boys act like they do because they were created in the image of a warrior God. There is no drug or other tool of man that can change what is written on their aggressive little hearts when they were formed in the womb.

If you are not blessed with an educator in your household, let me ask you this: Have you ever gone to a birthday party of a child under the age of six? If you want to see the image of God as a warrior, just observe the boys at the party. Boys will throw cake, stick their hands in the punch bowl, shove each other down, and about any other wild thing that can happen will more than likely be caused by them. As the parent of one of them, it is sometimes embarrassing when they act this way. But we have to pause for a moment and think about it from a biblical point of view: What we are seeing is the raw image of God and his nature that is best demonstrated by young boys in their wildest moments.

Why? Is there something wrong with boys these days or has it always been that way. I've got news for you, it has always been that way and will until the end of time. The reason being, God created boys in his image (remember He is a fearless warrior) and he set in them a fearless warrior soul. Boys act like boys because that is how they are wired by the Great Electrician because they are needed to bring order to this violent world. In essence, God created all boys to become heroes. Now I'm not saying he destined all of them to earn the Congressional Medal of Honor, but he did set within each of them the desire to come through. We were made to be the champions of our family, our work, and most of all for the Kingdom.

But what happens later on in life, does this desire for greatness depart from us? Praise God the answer is no simply because it can't. It is as much a part of us as our fingers and toes because it was branded upon our hearts by God. It is always there, sitting quietly on the bench of your heart waiting to be put into the game. Sometimes, it shows up in odd ways as we get older and become more conservative with our actions. I know in my life, the older I get, the less I am interested in taking risks like I did as a younger man. Instead of taking risks, many men turn their attention to other outlets to nurture this part of them that longs for adventure and risk.

Did you ever wonder why so many men are consumed with watching football, NASCAR, and boxing? Did you ever watch the actions of the men that live their lives through their children's sporting endeavors? Most men use these events as an attempt to fill the void left in them that was once occupied by the childhood sports and games we played such as saving the day as a soldier, a knight, or a cowboy. As we grow older, life happens and we quit doing the dangerous things like playing sports and settle into a more comfortable existence. Sure we may play on a softball team or hit the links for a day to help appease the desire for excitement, but it can never be completely snuffed out. Remember, these desires of our hearts are the very nature of God. He is a competitor, a fighter, a risk taker, and above all a warrior.

I am as guilty as any other man when it comes to finding an outlet for adventure through watching sports. When I watch baseball, part of me is twelve years old again and catching in little league. I know that if I put on the catcher's gear today and played I would really feel it the next day and probably the whole week. But, when I'm sitting on my couch watching a game, I'm in the game and living the dream, even if it is only in my mind.

Men have been wrapped up in sports for a long time. If you want proof of this, read the Apostle Paul's letters to the Churches and look for sports references. Obviously, Paul was a sports fan. In the letters he wrote to the Churches in Greek and Roman societies, he used sports terms to explain Christian principles. He urged them to "run the race" and he often spoke of wrestling and boxing.

Did you ever wonder why Paul used sports metaphors when he talked to the Churches? For one thing, he was a guy and he was writing to other guys. But the greatest reason for this is that the cultures he wrote to way back then were much like present day America in that they were all wrapped up in sports. Much like today, the great athletes of Paul's time were given a god-like status in society. Paul got down onto the same level with these cultures that would have clearly understood what he meant when he said "Run the race".

Paul sure new his audience as God guided his hands to craft some of the greatest books ever written. If he were alive and writing today, do you think he would change anything in his writing style? I think not because men are no different today than they were two thousand years ago.

Many men just like you and I, use the television to fill this need to play like we did as boys. Now that we have an unlimited amount of networks to choose from, it's easy to find a sporting event or a game show of some type to watch 24 hours a day. But not all men have a love of sports. Many men get hooked on their careers where they can compete against others to climb the corporate ladder to success. Some men find that trading stocks gives them an adrenaline rush and an element of danger. Regardless of the outlet men use, it all boils down to the fact that we were created to be aggressive, adventurous beings, just like our God.

There is a spiritual danger to our outlets for adventure that we must be aware of at all times. We must be on guard because the Enemy and the flesh seek to pervert our need for excitement. Many men have succumbed to pornography as their outlet for excitement while others become involved in sexual affairs. Remember, the Enemy and his army are continually patrolling around the perimeter looking for a weakness to exploit in order to distance you from God. If there is a weakness that the Enemy can pervert, you can rest assured he will try to, all the while convincing you that everything is A-Ok. All men need to take a long look at themselves and see what they use to bring excitement to their lives and ask themselves if it brings glory to God.

As we grow older, the Enemy's daily and often times subtle attacks on us, seems to disconnect us from our warrior soul. Think about it, how many times have you chosen to take the path of least resistance in life? Have you ever had a problem arise where you were faced with a conflict, but you let it go so you didn't have to fight it out? I'll be the first one to admit I have looked the other way instead of getting into a fight on several occasions. What I didn't realize was that I was playing into the Enemy's hand.

Most times we write conflicts off as petty issues that don't really matter. When we do this, what we are really doing is weakening our heart and suppressing the warrior soul that God created and pronounced good and pleasing in his sight. When we run from a fight, it is not only cowardly but it grieves our Creator that gave us the spirit of boldness. If that was not enough, when you run the first time, running gets easier each time, and pretty soon, you've lost heart and self-confidence and are a weakened man.

Think about Samson the Nazirite. He was by far the strongest man that ever lived and a champion for God, set apart at his birth. He was seduced by the lovely Delilah and tricked into telling her the source of his strength. It's easy to draw a parallel between Delilah and Satan. Satan is always trying to get us to show him what makes us weak so he can devise a plan to take us out. We pick up the story in Chapter 16 of Judges:

> "With such nagging she prodded him day after day until he was tired to death. So he told her everything. "No razor has ever been used on my head," he said, "because I am a Nazirite set apart to God since birth. If my head were shaved, my strength would leave me, and I would become as weak as any other man." (Judges 16:16-17)

You probably know the rest of the story, she lulled him to sleep and had him shaved bald. When he awoke his great strength was gone. Unlike Samson, we must remain awake and be aware that the Enemy is constantly attempting to lull us to sleep so he can cut off our hair. Since we were all set apart for God, we are no different than Sampson. We must be ever sober and vigilant at all times if we are to stand up to his schemes.

If you are finding yourself feeling like a weak man today, its never too late to start getting your strength back. The first thing you have to do is let your hair grow out (in the spiritual sense of course). Your hair will grow in thick and full if you use this natural hair tonic: Stop running and speak up! Don't be afraid to say what is on your heart. After all, you are armed with the sword of the Spirit. But the harsh reality is most men are worried they will fail and look like a loser in the eyes of other men. I'm not recommending you go looking for a fight, but if it takes sticking your neck out a little bit, do it. God wants to give you the strength that you need and He wants to give it to you directly from his hand. This is shown in Psalms when David said:

"When I called, you answered me; you made me bold and stouthearted" (Psalms 138:3)

He is all powerful and also all knowing. He knows when you are weak and he even knows what strength he needs to give you. All you have to do is ask. But how will he send it to us? One way is through the Holy Spirit as shown in Ephesians 3:16:

"I pray that out of his glorious riches he may strengthen you with power through his Spirit in your inner being" (Ephesians 3:16)

Another way God sends us strength is through the power of Christ. Paul new this first hand when he wrote:

"But the Lord stood at my side and gave me strength, so that through me the message might be fully proclaimed and all the Gentiles might hear it. And I was delivered from the lion's mouth" (II Tim 4:17)

There's that lion reference again. Christ will strengthen us and help us overcome any obstacle that Satan may throw in our path. Remember, Jesus is interceding for us right now! We need constant help from the Trinity of the Father, Son, and Holy Spirit to survive in this world that is controlled by Satan. We also need help from other Christian men that will walk beside us and share their strength. Jesus himself said to Peter:

"But I have prayed for you, Simon, that your faith may not fail. And when you have turned back, strengthen your brothers." (Luke 22:32)

Other Christian men that you can lean on are vital to your daily walk There is an old saying that "No man is an island" and that rings true throughout the Christian world. In an earlier chapter I told you how the lion hunts by isolating it's prey from the pack. Don't be that isolated one, you need other men to fight for you and they need you as well. Christian men can grow strong when they fight for each other as a group all the while sharing wisdom and power with each other.

When I started training my Golden Retriever to sit and shake hands, I called my Dad to ask for some advice. When he was a young man, my Dad bred and trained dogs and I wanted to tap into his wisdom and draw strength from him in the matter. I remember him telling me that to train a dog to do what you desire is actually teaching the dog a habit, developed through repetition. I learned this was true because after about seven days of practicing "Sit", Napoleon sat!

Your spirit of boldness is no different in that if you use it repetitively, it will soon become second nature. And when this happens, you can really start to live your life without fear. That is, as long as you remember this one little rule: "Don't worry about what someone else may think". So many times, men are bogged down by the worry of how they may look or how their image may be tarnished. Men, you must set the pace in your life and get over yourself! Everyone around you needs to see clearly who you are, where you stand, and that they are just going to have to deal with it. Take my word, you will thank yourself later for doing this today because it will put you on the road to living from your spirit of boldness.

I've tried to get to the root cause of why Christian men exist in such a weak state and I tend to always blame it on the flesh and the Enemy. However, there is another area to point a finger at and that is the popular culture. We internalize and accept the pop culture ideas and institutions that we continually see on television, read in the press, and hear on the radio. Just like my Golden Retriever learning to sit, we are being told how we should act, talk, look, and behave. In other words, we are having the wishes of the media *gently* rammed down our throats. I stress the word gently because we are being indoctrinated slowly with spoon-fed information in the most subtle way possible; through television portraying men badly. And we are starting to pay for it in a big way.

The common trend that I have noticed in today's movies, sitcoms, and commercials is this: Men are stupid, bumbling fools that can't get anything right so they should be laughed at and never taken seriously. In fact, Hollywood (or Hollyweird as I like to call it) has been on the "Dumb Dad" kick for quite some time. Shows that portray men in a negative light have been around long enough that the up and coming generation is starting to accept them as the way men really are. This acceptance of a false truth is scary and is harming men by putting them on the same level of performing circus chimps.

When I asked myself why would Hollywood choose to portray men in this light, I am reminded of the Saturday Night Live skit the Church Lady, and her famous line "Could it be..........Satan????" Yes Church Lady, sadly, you may be on to something because Satan loves to use the media to invade our homes by way of a coaxial cable.

Satan knows there is power in you and he also knows that with God on your side, he cannot defeat you. His greatest fear is that men will unite and come against him in the name of Christ. This is what he fears and tries to keep from happening. For too long men's swords have dulled and rusted. I've got good news for you, it's sharpening time!

Chapter 5
Iron Sharpening Iron

The sword is single handedly the most important weapon ever developed. No other weapon
has shaped history like the sword. Kingdoms were
built and destroyed by way of this perfect weapon. In
literary circles, the sword symbolizes valor, bravery,
honor, and most of all danger. There is a mystical
quality of swords and some people even go so far
as to believe that swords possess their own person-
alities. Historians are unsure of when the first sword
was crafted and it is also unknown how long ago one
was first drawn in offense. Through the ages and up
to today, the sword is first and foremost the universal
symbol of the warrior craft.

The art of sword crafting requires years of diligent study and supervised experience. The sword
maker (or bladesmith) begins crafting a sword by
first heating a piece of raw steel in a forge to around
900° Fahrenheit. At this temperature, the steel will

glow bright orange and is now malleable enough to begin the process of shaping. Shaping a sword is done by continually pounding on it in order to "draw out" the steel into a longer and flatter piece. At some point, the bladesmith will fold the steel back over onto itself and reheat it to assure a good weld. Then the process is repeated and the blade is redrawn and flattened out. This will be continued until the bladesmith is pleased with the steel's strength and size. When satisfied, the bladesmith will begin shaping the sword into the desired final pattern. This is a crucial step in the process for the bladesmith because he must be sure to keep the steel hot enough to shape into the intended design but also cool enough to avoid cracking. If the temperature of the blade is off by a few degrees, the blade may become brittle and crack and the process must be started over.

After the blade is shaped, it is cooled to preserve its lines. But the work is far from over, the hardest part comes next. The bladesmith will now taper the blade in order to create the tip and tang of the blade by hammering the steel at an angle. This is a painstaking process and requires continued heating and flipping of the blade. The angle of the blade must be maintained and must perfectly match the opposite side of the sword.

Throughout the tapering process, the bladesmith must take breaks from hammering in order to normalize the blade. Normalizing is done by heating the blade to glowing hot inside a forge and then removing it and allowing the blade to air cool without doing anything to it. Normalizing is vital to the strength of the crystalline structure of the steel that is changed each time the bladesmith hammers it. By allowing the blade to be heated and cooled, the grain of the steel is aloud to "smooth itself out".

Once tapered and normalized, the blade is annealed. Annealing is similar to normalizing in that the blade is heated up to the appropriate temperature to allow it to austenize (carbon and iron molecules mix). However, annealing is a much slower process. The blade is evenly heated and allowed to cool very slowly. In fact, annealing a blade may take up to a full day. Annealing is the most important step in the entire process because it assures the proper mixing of the steel's atoms which gives it hardness and prepares the blade for tempering.

Tempering is begun by heating the blade up yet again. However, this time the blade is not heated to the point that austenization occurs, but to a much lower temperature. The blade is kept at this temperature for a while, then it is quenched in water. Most bladesmiths temper a blade several times to get the exact level of hardness. The idea is that the metal is hard enough to maintain an edge but not so hard that it is brittle and susceptible to chipping and cracking.

Once the blade is tempered, the blade is painstakingly sharpened to perfection. After sharpening, most swords are decorated in various ways depending on the sword's intended use. Normally the crafter will add his finishing touches in the way of embossing the blade, personalizing it, or adding decorations. When complete, the bladesmith will sign his work that will forever show that he created, sculpted, and completed a masterpiece of artwork that is also an instrument of death.

Sword crafting is an intense, tiring, and stressful process that may take several days to complete a sword that is ready for battle. Every step of sword making has to be precise or the steel will become flawed and possibly break. Due to the difficulty and the pains they endure, Bladesmiths will tell you they do not make swords, they give birth to them.

You can draw a parallel between the Christian man and the sword. The Christian man is like raw steel that must be shaped and sharpened in order to turn out a fine product. The Bible tells us this fact when it was written:

"As iron sharpens iron, so one man sharpens another" (Proverbs 27:17)

What God is telling us in this passage is that it takes other men to help you along the road of your spiritual journey. Only other men can help you "sharpen" yourself and keep you motivated as you grow strong in the Spirit. There is no instruction manual that you can turn to, and you need others that have been there to use as references. Other brothers can lift you up, pray with and for you, walk with you, and most of all help expose weaknesses you may not have noticed so that you can be strengthened.

Whoa! You just said "Expose weaknesses"! Yes I did and believe it or not it is vital to your walk with Christ. Every man carries weaknesses that he either chooses to ignore or he simply fails to see because he chooses to ignore them. It's kind of like my when my son uses what I like to refer to as "selective hearing". This occurs when I am only be a few feet away and speaking directly to him. It's pretty obvious when I say something that he doesn't like because he acts as if he had never heard a word I said. He just goes on about his business, ignoring me all the while. He is only performing an exercise in bluffing by selecting not to listen. When other men come along side us, they have an unobstructed view and can see the things we either fail to see (or choose not to) that are often in their line of sight. Also, other Christian men are often prompted by the Holy Spirit to help us expose what may be wrong in our spiritual walk and bring it to your attention.

A while back, out of the blue, my friend Roy in Florida emailed me to ask if there was anything I may be hanging on to that could be holding me back and keeping me from God's intended blessing. He told me in his message that he felt lead by the Holy Spirit to ask me if there was a thought process, habit, or some other sin that was keeping me from being the man God designed me to be. When I replied to his email, the first thing I did was thank him for following the lead of the Spirit. The next thing I did was explain to him how I have recently been wrestling with a prideful spirit. This battle has involved me wanting credit for everything that I do instead of glorifying God. I told him that I know in my heart I need to glorify God but lately I have wanted a piece of the action. Does that sound like the flesh or what? By him coming to me and asking me this tough question it lead to a great turning point in my life and in authoring this book. It made me realize that many things I have done lately have been self centered and all about me. I immediately started praying that God would use me in a mighty way to bring him all the credit and applause that I have desired for myself. In that case, my friend's iron sharpened me a little more.

This is precisely what God had in mind from the beginning: Men leaning on other men for strength and support. One of my favorite examples of this in the Bible is the relationship between the brothers Joab and Abishai found in II Samuel Chapter 10. Joab was a General in King David's army and was dispatched to defeat the Ammonites and the Arameans. After essentially leading his men into a fighting position where they were surrounded, Joab put his brother Abishai in charge of the bulk of his troops to fight the Ammonites on one front, while he took a group of the finest warriors with him to fight on the other side of the battlefield against the Arameans. Both of these men were in a life and death situation and they knew it. They were outnumbered, cut off, and surrounded. But, because of their brotherly bond, they drew strength from each other by pledging to watch each other's back, as found in the following verses:

> "Joab said, "If the Arameans are too strong for me, then you are to come to my rescue; but if the Ammonites are too strong for you, then I will come to rescue you. Be strong and let us fight bravely for our people

and the cities of God. The Lord will do what is good in his sight." (II Sam 10:11-12)

The rest of the story goes on to tell how the Ammonites and the Aramean Armies facing Joab and Abishai's troops ran from the field of battle, retreating to the area around Helam. That's when David took the rest of the army of Israel, crossed the Jordan and destroyed all of them.

The brothers Joab and Abishai pledged to be there for each other and fight bravely. They did as they promised and were victorious not only for their own troops but their bravery ultimately lead to total victory for the King. This is what we must keep our eyes focused on: When we sharpen each other by fighting alongside one another, we are ultimately taking ground for a larger cause and inching toward victory for our King, Jesus.

But, is it possible to sharpen too much? I learned that it is possible when I was only ten years old. That was when I bought my first knife at the flea market. It was a lock-blade variety made in Pakistan and I carried it everywhere. Whenever I had it in my pocket, I felt dangerous. I wasn't just another little boy, I had a weapon that could bring down any enemy that got in my way. I couldn't have hurt anyone with it in real life, but in my mind I was the bravest kid on the block. When I was bored, I would sharpen the knife on a sharpening stone that my Dad had taught me to use. I sharpened my knife so much that I eventually ruined the blade. In fact, I made it dull and in such bad shape that it would not cut through warm butter.

Just like the "fine" knives from Pakistan, men can also be sharpened too much. The Church has devised a solution for making men stronger by telling them to read the right books, take spirituality seminars, and discipleship classes. I will be the first one to agree that the knowledge gained from these sorts of things is nice and all Christian topics are important to study. But more times than not, all I see are men taking classes and not putting into action what they are given by God!

It seems as though today's Church has men so busy sharpening that they never look up long enough to even see the battle going on around them, let alone engage in it. I know this for a fact because I have been there. Every time I finished yet another class/book/seminar, I was left with the thought "Ok, what do I do now?". Most times I would go searching online for the next, newest thing out there in book form that would help me be the man that I thought I needed to be. I would order it, read it, take copious notes, and then file them away with all the rest of the books in my bookcase. Little did I know I was right in the middle of the vicious cycle of sharpening myself to a blunt, dull edge. I didn't realize that what I gained in knowledge, I lost in spirituality.

The best way I can relate this to my never ending cycle of sharpening is in a quote the great Groucho Marx once said:

"The only problem with doing nothing is you never know when you're done."

Well, I never new I was finished with that cycle until I started getting my notes together and drafted the outline for this book. That's when I realized the cycle had been defeated and I was now free to run with the warrior spirit of boldness that God wrote on my heart.

When I started the research for this book, I realized that in order to be truly sharpened and honed into a warrior for the Kingdom, men need each other's *spiritual kinship* to bestow knowledge to each other. I define spiritual kinship as relating to others on a spiritual and emotional level where knowledge is shared and relationships are built. It is only through this spiritual relationship with other men that we can be equally equipped for the Army of God and essentially go through Boot Camp together. What men don't need is another class about all the areas where they have been failing.

I know I am not alone in this feeling because I've heard many other men express this same concern like in the following statement from an anonymous Christian man:

"For the first time in a while, I feel hope again. I was educated in a Christian school, attended Church twice a week, was involved with the youth group, and went on mission trips. And yet, as an adult, when "real life" hit me with the realities of pain, loss, unexplainable trials, etc, I kept doing the things I thought I should. I attended the Bible meetings, said the right things, prayed what I thought were the right prayers - all to no avail.

I kept sharpening my sword but nothing happened. I suppose you could say that rather than use my sword, or vainly keep sharpening it, I dropped it. Because I forgot what it was for, what my purpose is for. I was walking blindly in the midst of the battle-field wondering why things weren't working. Why God wasn't working. I haven't got it all figured out yet. But I am picking up my sword again. And when I start to sharpen - it will be to use it." -Anonymous

If you see yourself in this man's words, you are not alone. In fact, I would guess that most Christian men feel this way deep down inside. It is no doubt the author of the above statement is a Christian in a daily battle like we all are. The thing that strikes me hardest about his statement is that he did all the "Religious Stuff" and couldn't figure out why he wasn't getting anywhere. He obviously had a reve-lation and realized he had done the religious/tradi-tional things but had not taken up the spiritual part and lived from his heart.

When we do things spiritually and get rid of the religiosity in our lives, we can really start to gain ground for God. So many times we get bogged down on religion and traditions and miss the big picture of what is really going on around us. Our spiritual swords are what we fight with in this world against the darkness and principalities of evil. Like a blade-smith filing a newly formed sword, we need other men to help us reveal the areas of our spiritual life, expose them, and sharpen them by relating battle experience to one another. The great Theologian C.S. Lewis wrote:

> "We are born helpless....We need others physically, emotionally, intellectually: we need them if we are to know anything, even ourselves".

The strength of relationships that we build with others is the only way we can even hope to survive the battle for our souls. This battle rages around us at all times and we must become a soldier and "get in the fight". Actually, when you became a Christian, you signed the papers and raised your right hand, so to speak. The only problem is, most men find themselves sitting around waiting to ship off to boot camp while the battle rages around them. If you've never been a soldier, there are a few books out and even a movie that follows the lives of soldiers that fought in Mogadishu, Somalia in the early 1990's. These men were immortalized as heroes in the halls of military history by running the "Mogadishu Mile". If their story is new to you, I'll attempt to set the stage:

> A group of Army Rangers and a Delta Force Commando have been fighting their way through the bullet ridden streets of Mogadishu on foot. Death and destruction are everywhere, they are outnumbered, outgunned, and they have no way to get back to the safety of the American Compound. They try to hitch

a ride out in armored vehicles of a convoy of UN Peacekeeping Armored vehicles. But guess what, they're all full. All that's left to do is run and run they do, all the while taking constant fire from enemy forces. So here they are, men in full combat dress running down a street of a third world nation all the time taking fire and engaging the enemy as they run. The good news is, they all make it back to the American safe area alive and in one piece. Through unimaginable odds, these soldiers banded together and made it.

There has never been a time more crucial than today that men are needed to rise up and lock arms with one another in God's Army and fight like the soldiers described here. Men are only sharpened when they engage the enemy with their spiritual swords. I'm sure you've heard that there is strength in numbers haven't you? This is as true in the spiritual realm as it is in the physical because when groups of men come together against the enemy in the name of Jesus, the power of God is released!

You may be saying to yourself, "Wow Donny, thanks for the pep-talk, but I just don't have the ability to bring men together like this". Guess what….. neither do I, but God does! If you are reading this book, it is obvious that God has given you a passion for helping men grow in Him and come alive to the abundant life He has promised. He wants you to succeed and will give you what you need to go the distance. So, how do we get started? We first have to pay a visit to the Great Outfitter.

What's the first thing you do before setting off on an adventure into the wild? You go see an Outfitter! The Outfitter has the "stuff" you need for your trip and can set you up with tents, backpacks, and whatever else you need to take. More importantly, he is also an expert and can show you things you will need that you may not have thought about.

As Christians, we have an inside track because God is the Great Outfitter of life. He has ALL the gear that we need and He is more than generous to give it away. Every person that accepts Christ as their savior has just signed on for a great adventure comparable to an epic odyssey. In this adventure there will be beautiful vistas from the mountaintop, dreary times in the valley, and a villain that is stalking us. Not to worry though, God is there to guide us on our journey and stock our spiritual knapsacks with wisdom along the way. For a good example of this, read about my hero Moses. Moses stuttered his speech and was a lousy shepherd. In fact, he couldn't keep up with his sheep let alone lead them. But, as usual, God came through and equipped Moses into a powerful speaker and fearless leader. And then there was Peter, Andrew, James, and John that only new of nets and fish but God equipped them. And the good news today is, He's still in the equipping business.

Other men around you will help sharpen you but the final razor sharp edge can only be put on you by God himself. This is done as you walk beside Him and become outfitted by His grace. The catch is, just like Moses and the simple fishermen, you must be willing go wherever it is that He leads you because there is no one else on earth that God created to do the job He has designed you for. He knows where you need to be at every given moment to fulfill His work. Because so much is riding on your life, He will not abandon you and He will walk beside of you every step of the way teaching you as you go. He longs to give you wisdom and strength. But, the most important of all the gifts he can give you is his presence. When the presence of God is with you, you are more than a conqueror. To prove it, here is what God's word tells us:

"Have I not commanded you? Be strong and courageous. Do not be terrified; do not be discouraged, for the Lord your God will be with you wherever you go". (Joshua 1:9)

The presence of God is what drives the Christian man onward and upward in his daily walk. It is also more than that, it is life. David knew this when he wrote:

"Those who are far from you will perish; you destroy all who are unfaithful to you. But as for me, it is good to be near God. I have made the Sovereign Lord my refuge; I will tell of all your deeds" (Psalms 73:27-28)

David is referred to as "A man after God's heart" and it is obvious here that he was very close to Him.

If we gain anything from David's knowledge it is this: If you try to go it alone outside of Gods presence, you are being unfaithful to Him and you will not and cannot make it. You must have God's presence in your life if you are to ever be equipped by Him for the journey He has marked out for you from the beginning of time.

If you would have told me five years ago I would write a book about men forming a warrior culture that fights together for the Kingdom, I would have probably laughed in your face. But today, I can tell you that what I write here comes from my heart and that I didn't have the experience, the words, or the knowledge I've shared with you until now. God has equipped me as I have walked with Him and allowed Him to take over my life. Sure, I still have the fleshly moments when I slip up, but the great thing is, He never stops equipping us! I look forward to the future because I know I will continue to grow in His knowledge as long as I keep asking for it.

As I mentioned, equipping is a never-ending, life long process. You might be saying, "Oh great, I'll never be ready.", but that is simply not the case. You don't have to wait all your life to join the battle. It has been said that maturity in the Christian life belongs to those who know they're not yet mature. In other words, it is reserved for those who know they still have a lot to learn and a long way to go. The Christian warrior is needed now! When you triumphantly march onto the field of battle, you will be sharpened and equipped from the moment you draw your sword to fight.

So what does the picture of a Christian warrior that has been sharpened and is ready for battle look like? The good news is that his characteristics are not something I made up for this book and I didn't learn them from a Professor of Theology. As a matter of fact, there is no mystery to them at all. All of them are in black and white in your Bible! You have probably even read them before and maybe even written some of them down for later study. But what you may have missed was how to use them in this context. And that context is living life as a spiritual warrior.

First and foremost, the Christian Warrior has to be armored up everyday. We do this by asking for and putting on the full armor of God. Paul explains this in chapter six of Ephesians when he said:

> "Finally, be strong in the Lord and in his mighty power. Put on the full armor of God so that you can take your stand against the Devil's schemes. For our struggle is not against flesh and blood, but against rulers, against the authorities, against the powers of this dark world and against the spiritual forces of evil in the heavenly realms." (Eph 6:10-12).

Plain and simple, the Devil is out to get us and our only protection comes from the strength of the Lord our God. Paul lays out the landscape of the battle-field when he tells us that we do not fight against humans but our enemies are supernatural evil forces. Remember, Satan is the ruler of this world and his emissaries are constantly patrolling around your perimeter looking for a weakness to strike at. It's a good thing for us that our God is there with us and is willing to provide and outfit us with the ultimate protection, His armor.

"Therefore, put on the full armor of God, so that when the day of evil comes, you may be able to stand your ground, and after you have done everything, to stand" (Eph 6:13)

There it is, my favorite part! The armor protects us from the onslaught of evil aimed at taking us out. I love how Paul says "and after you have done everything", in other words fought your heart out, "to stand", as in Victory! This is the quintessential perfect example of standing your ground in battle, slugging it out with the Enemy, defeating him, and ultimately being the last man standing, or the "King of the Hill", so to speak. Paul goes on to explain the armor in detail:

"Stand firm then, with the belt of truth buckled around your waist, with the breastplate of righteousness in place, and with your feet fitted with the readiness that comes from the gospel of peace. In addition to all this, take up the shield of faith, with which you can extinguish all the flaming arrows of the evil one. Take the helmet of salvation......." (Eph 6: 14-17a)

Did you notice that up until now, all of these items are defensive weaponry? Each of the aforementioned are used to keep you intact while you fight so you can keep going. But finally, here is the offensive part:

"and the sword of the Spirit, which is the word of God" (Eph 6: 17b)

Unlike the sword crafted from a piece of steel by a bladesmith, the sword we use to fight evil is alive. Hebrews 4:12 tells us:

"For the Word of God is <u>living</u> and <u>active</u>. Sharper than any double-edged sword, it penetrates even to dividing soul and spirit, joints and marrow; it judges the thoughts and attitudes of the heart" (Heb 4:12)

The Word of God alive! The living Word is also stronger than anything Satan can dish out and any problem that will ever be set before us on the table of life. His living Word is by far His greatest gift.

Throughout the Bible we see examples of God's unbelievable faithfulness and our constant rejection of Him. I can't even begin to fathom how He can remain so in love with us given all of the heartache we have incurred upon Him. I guess it's because He is God and I am not and most of all, He can see the big picture because He is the artist that painted it.

It is no doubt that if we could see like Him, we would be ashamed at our behavior. While we are out chasing after things that have no value in the Kingdom

Marriage can be a tough undertaking. Men and women are completely different. Communication, love languages, and compromise are all very complicated.

There's something for everyone in this series. We'll apply personal situations and hard core truths to the lies society leads us to believe about love and relationships.

We look forward to having you and your friends join us for this series as we talk about why "its Complicated".

Meeting at
Riverbend High School
Sundays @ 9:30 & 11:15
www.visitlifepoint.org

of Heaven, He is there patiently calling to us. And to beat it all, God sent His only son to die for us so that we could come to Him! Jesus died for you, me, your friends at work, Osama Bin Laden, and every other person on Earth. But how could he send His only son to die such a horrible death for us? From the human standpoint, I know for a fact that there is no way I would allow a hair on my son's head to be harmed for the sake of someone else, especially someone who had continually thumbed their nose in my face. But then again, that is the fleshly, human perspective. The fact of the matter is, He is God and we cannot fathom or even come close to understanding His thoughts or the boundless love He has for us.

But God not only sent His son into this world so we could come to Him, He also gave us his Holy Spirit. The Holy Spirit is our counselor and teacher that enlightens us to God's wants and desires. When we become a Christian, we are given a pure heart where the Holy Spirit takes up residence. We talked about the Holiest Place in a previous chapter, and I'm sure you've heard the saying, "Your body is the temple". With that said, live like it! God lives inside of you, walks with you, and goes everywhere and sees everything. There is no hiding anything from Him.

You were given the Holy Spirit to be your guide through all of the trials and temptations of this evil world. I can sleep at night knowing that His Spirit is in my heart and is ever changing and counseling me. What excites me the most is that I am carrying around inside of me an all powerful, all knowing entity that has already overcome the world! With that said, I feel that it is our call to duty to wield this gift against our very real and powerful Enemy through prayer. Paul gives us some more insight into how to fight when he penned:

"And pray in the Spirit on all occasions with all kinds of requests." (Eph 6:18)

Pray first to be filled with the Holy Spirit then ask for whatever sincere need you may have. Pray for yourself, your friends, your neighbors, the guy at the grocery store, against afflictions, to bind evil spirits, just pray for everything. Don't get hung up on how your prayer may sound. Quite simply – Pray, Pray, Pray! Or better yet I should say Fight! Fight!! Fight!!!

This leads me to the primary characteristic of a Christian Warrior and that is he loves to Fight! (woops) What I meant to say was **pray**. Actually fighting and praying are the same thing when you get right down to it. If you need an example, think of prayer and how it compares with boxing. The boxer gets in the ring with an opponent and starts trading blows. Eventually, he becomes tired and weak from all of the fighting. Also, if his opponent is any good, he will have identified a weak spot and attempted to exploit it by continually jabbing at it. When we intercede for others, we are putting our self in the ring for that person. We are the one giving out the licks. Remember, there is strength in numbers and the more people fighting for you, the better chance you have at snatching victory.

Christian warriors must be steadfast in prayer and they must also be cunning enough to avoid worldly entanglements. The Apostle Paul wrote to his understudy Timothy:

> "Endure hardship with us like a good soldier of Christ Jesus. No one serving as a soldier gets involved in civilian affairs- he wants to please his commanding officer"(II Tim 2:3-4)

The Enemy seeks to distract you from your mission. If he can use the worldliness of other people he will. How many times have you set out to accomplish something but were shot down by others? I know I have, and I'm sure you are not a stranger to this. In fact, one time I was all geared up and ready to start a business. I had done my homework, checked out the local need for it, and started my training. When I shared my desire with one of my most trusted friends, he told me quite simply that it would never work and that I was wasting my time. As you can imagine, I soon abandoned the business idea and went on with life. The Enemy has a way of casting doubt in our mind and he will often try to do this through people we place high a value on. So once again, be on the lookout.

One of the most difficult of all things a soldier must do is to deny their self. This is hard for the average male not only because of pride, but also because most of us have gone through our whole lives living from our minds. We analyze everything that happens with our brains and, "Think things through", while we should be living from our hearts. God has provided us with the Holy Spirit to dwell in our hearts, counsel us, and lead us in this world. He did this so that we can more easily say NO to the things of this world. The Bible tells us:

> "For the grace of God that brings salvation has appeared to all men. It teaches us to say "No' to ungodliness and worldly passions, and to live self-controlled, upright and godly lives in this present age." (Titus 2:11,12)

Denying self and dieing to self is not a choice, it is a commandment. We must put away our methods and agendas and receive from God what he has in store for us. Do you really think you are smarter than Him?

But, it doesn't end there because all soldiers need physical and mental endurance to overcome the daily battles in their lives. They must also be conditioned to rise up and fight even when battle weary. James tells us:

> "Blessed is the man who perseveres under trial, because when he has stood the test, he will receive the crown of life that God has promised to those who love him." (James 2:12)

We have a reward waiting for us, all we have to do is finish the race. Now that race is not an easy one and has many hills to climb. But keep in mind that life is not a sprint, it is a marathon that requires pace rather than speed.

When you became a Christian your name was written on the muster sheets of God's Army. The battle for you began long ago and will continue for the rest of your days on Earth. This will require great self control on your part. Self control is simply the way you exert your own will on your personal self. Or in other words, it is how you behave, act, and think. Paul wrote about self control when he penned:

> "So then, let us not be like others, who are asleep, but let us be self-controlled........ putting on faith and love as a breastplate, and the hope of salvation as a helmet." (I Thess 5:6 and 8)

Self control and discipline work hand in hand. It takes both to be able to keep your wits about yourself while in battle. Keeping your wits enhances your alertness and makes you ready to stand your ground. We've got God's word on it that if we resist Satan, he must depart from you.

> "Resist him (the Devil), standing firm in the faith, because you know that your brothers throughout the world are undergoing the same kind of sufferings." (I Pet 5:9)

and

"Submit yourselves, then, to God. Resist the Devil and he will flee from you" (James 4:7)

God has been more than generous by providing us with everything we could possibly need to fight with. It is up to us to incorporate them into our daily lives so that they may become second nature. One Christian warrior can change the world for God, but when several come together, the power of God is released by the bucketfuls.

Chapter 6
Creating A Warrior Culture

What is a warrior culture? You may have pictures in your head of knights, Barbarians, Vikings, or any number of things that your imagination can cook up. Since I was a soldier once, I like to relate it to my military experience where I was surrounded by dangerous men that were trained to kill. As a matter of fact, I never felt more secure in my life than when I was with my comrades and we were all going "down range" in our tank. When you are with other fighting men, you know what you have been trained to do and you can rest assured that your buddy next to you knows what to do as well. Confidence in the man next to you is a source of strength for you to draw from and ultimately use to complete your mission. This dependence on the guy next to you is the glue that binds entire armies together.

All of my life, I have been fascinated with military history, especially tactics and strategy. One of my favorite tacticians that I have studied is Shaka Zulu. Shaka was a revolutionary tactician that changed the face of warfare in tribal Africa in the late 1700's. Prior to his arrival on the scene, warfare was carried out by local Chiefs through empty taunts and threats of battle. When a war was declared, the Chief would march his band of warriors onto the battlefield. Each warrior would carry one long spear that was designed for throwing. The battle would begin with each side taunting the other with offensive gestures, dancing, and screaming. Attacks were limited to throwing spears from long range that rarely struck down their intended opponent. Battles would end after each side grew tired of dancing and taunting and each would leave the battlefield for the comforts of their village where they would celebrate victory. As you can see, little was accomplished by either side.

Thus came the entrance of Shaka Zulu. Shaka was a charismatic leader that recognized the need for change in the tribal methods of warfare. He was dynamic in that he conceived the short, stabbing spear (the Iklwa) and the larger heavier shield made of cowhide that was carried by his warriors. These tools of the trade were designed for close quarters fighting and he trained his men to use them through constant drilling and training.

Shaka put an end to the pseudo-warfare that had been carried out for years between the tribes of Africa. Instead of taunting and dancing, the Zulu force would run in a Buffalo Horn (curved) formation toward the opponents ranks, encircle them, and then attack. The Zulu attack was carried out by thrusting their long shield into an enemy soldier's smaller shield, lifting the enemy's shield skyward exposing the ribs, and then plunging the iklwa into the naked ribs. The Zulu would continue this attack until every enemy soldier was dead or had run from the field of battle.

In just a few short years, the Zulu tribe under Shaka's direction rose in power and controlled the majority of southern Africa. The revolutionary tactics that Shaka taught his people were unmatched by any other tribe of the time not only because they had never been used, but because they became the lifestyle of the Zulu people. In fact, by the time a Zulu male was six years old, he was already an apprentice in the army charged with transporting supplies and supporting the rear areas. In essence, Shaka created and mandated a warrior culture. If you were born a Zulu it was inevitable that you would begin training for war as soon as you were old enough to walk around the village.

The Male Christian culture of today should take a lesson from the Zulu tribe if they are to break out of the mold Christian men have been shaped in. We must become like Shaka, not only by being revolutionary but also cunning enough to begin nurturing the next generation of warriors. Many times, I've seen men that claim to be warriors but in reality they are only dancing around taunting and not really engaging the enemy in warfare with sword and shield. It is time to be dynamic and get on the battlefield with the sole purpose of fighting and nothing else.

This leads me to the definition of a Christian *warrior culture*:

A warrior culture is a group of men that unite with one another to fight spiritual battles against evil. Fighting is their primary function and it becomes so ingrained in them that it is their second nature. These are men of God that will never give up, will always stick together, will fight fervently for each other, all the while watching each others backs, and will refuse to leave anyone behind to be picked off. They are in essence a mighty army of God that lays the groundwork and raises up future generations of warriors.

The warrior culture in our Churches today seems to be pretty much non-existent. Most Churches I have seen are still stuck in a funk much like tribal Africa, prior to Shaka's arrival. Although they may have good intentions, they are not being dynamic enough to raise up warriors for Christ. This archaic mindset tells us that men should get together once a month and eat, maybe play golf a couple of times a year, or come together and do some much needed grounds upkeep. Do you really think those accomplish anything? Or better yet, how on earth do they help men in the daily battle for their lives? I sometimes wonder if the leaders of today's Christian movement know the pulse of the average American Christian male that is living in the eight to five world, trying to pay his bills, and lead a household. Or, is it a male pride issue? Call it what you want but I can't help but think that the Church culture has been blind-sided by the Enemy in this area also.

One of the lies the Enemy has been very successful with lately is that men do not need to be pastored. Men need to go to Church, listen to a sermon, and fix things that break. Because men are creatures of comfort and don't normally like to step out of their comfort zones, they naturally will lay back with the attitude that someone else will do the work in the running the Church. After this ball is set in motion, you guessed it, the men have handed over the reigns of the Church to women. The landscape of most Churches consists of women doing almost everything because if they don't then who will? It seems that the climate of almost every Church I have entered involves women running almost all of the ministries. Now don't take me as a sexist, I am only stating what I have witnessed over the past decade. The thing that scares me the most about this type of system is that I believe by not developing our men, we are missing out on blessings that God wants to give not only to the Church but also to its families.

Most Churches only scratch the surface of the potential of Christian men when they start a so called "Men's Ministry". But praise the Lord that some Churches are willing to attempt starting one! The sad truth is, most Churches today do not have a ministry component that is totally devoted to building up the men of the body. Most have a ministry for children, students, and women but tend to discard men as not needing one. Biblically speaking, wasn't it set up by God that he would communicate to Jesus, then to the men, that communicate to women, and then to the children when Paul wrote:

> "Now I want you to realize that the head of every man is Christ, and the head of the woman is man, and the head of Christ is God." (1 Cor 11:3)

Men are a vital link in God's chain of communication. Without them "In the loop", we are bound to get our wires crossed and ultimately shorted out.

I want you to think about Stan and Dave from the earlier chapter for a moment. These two are a snapshot of the average Church going male. Sadly enough, Stan and Dave are at your Church every week. And even worse, Stan and Dave are going through their week alone, isolated, and ready to be picked off. What Stan and Dave need is a warrior mentality that will bond them together for battle. The problem is, they don't realize it because they have been blinded by the Enemy. Never is a community of warrior men serving each other more needed than today.

What we have been talking about here is how your daily walk depends not only on your relationship with God, but also your relationship and dependence on others that will go to war for you and watch your back. Remember, the enemy prowls like a roaring lion seeking to devour you. Do you remember how the lion hunts? He identifies the weakest animal in the pack, assaults the pack causing great flurry and confusion, isolates the weak animal from the pack, and pounces on and devours it. Men, we are in daily battle for our souls and need other men to help us along the way and prevent us from becoming isolated and ultimately devoured. So let me ask you this question: Who do you want watching your back, a nice Church guy at a potluck dinner or an army ranger with a machine gun that is itching to use it?

But the big question on your mind has to be, "How do we turn the ordinary Christian man into the extraordinary?" I'll start by saying that it all starts with training that all warriors must have prior to taking the battlefield. You can't hand a new recruit a rifle and a uniform and send him to the front line for duty. The new recruit must first go through basic training where he will learn how to do things the military way. But the greatest thing it teaches a recruit is how to survive in battle using team work. Most men don't understand how to fight with each other because they have never been afforded the opportunity to do so.

Up to this point, I have spent a lot of time talking about how men need each other in man to man relationships. Men need other men to walk with and help them along the way. However, the first step in training men to be warriors is that the individual man must be willing to be transformed. To be a warrior, the man must deny himself and walk with God trusting in his counsel only. I've told you that God will equip you as you walk with him. And to truly walk with God, you have to get alone with Him and let him speak to your heart. This is most evident in the life of St. Patrick who was a mighty warrior for God.

Most people are familiar with St. Patrick only because there is a holiday named for him. The thing I most remember that if you didn't wear green on St. Patrick's Day, it gave everybody an open invitation to pinch you. I've asked several people what they new about St. Patrick have gotten answers like, "He drove the snakes out of Ireland", and "Wasn't he a leprechaun?". Those are the most popular myths about him, but his life is one of the most significant of any Christian that ever lived.

St. Patrick was most likely born into a Christian family in present day England during the rule of the Roman Empire. When he was a young man, he was captured by slave traders and taken to Ireland. In Ireland, he was sold into slavery to a land owner that made him a Shepherd. Shepherds of this time lived in total isolation from the world and spent their days and nights in the wilderness watching after sheep and warding off attacks by wild animals.

God's hand was on St. Patrick and I'm sure he felt it because during his isolation, St. Patrick did not have anyone to talk to, so he prayed. It is said that he prayed without ceasing for six years in the wilderness. In this time, he developed a deep relationship with God and allowed God to equip him.

St. Patrick escaped slavery through a divine series of events and went on to study theology and was equipped with even more knowledge. He eventually returned to Ireland and was responsible for converting the country to Christianity.

St. Patrick's life is a testimony to how God can equip you as you walk with him and more importantly talk with him. We may not have the circumstances like St. Patrick but God is always there and His grace is sufficient for each of us. As I mentioned in the previous chapter, God will equip us like He equipped St. Patrick, if only we will walk with Him.

We must have a personal walk with God every day, every hour, minute, second.....you get the point. To really know God, we must surrender to Him, stop flying by the instruments in our minds, and start listening to our hearts. God is speaking to our hearts all the time hoping we will listen. It is crucial to our spiritual life that we turn up the volume of our hearts and turn down the knob for our minds. When we walk with God by listening to and living from our hearts, only then will we really get to know Him. And, only then can we be used by Him and be transformed into the warrior He intended us to be since time began.

To become a powerful warrior for his kingdom, we have to let Him change us on the inside. A way that He likes to work is by using other men of God to influence us. As you've already seen, there is strength in numbers and to be an affective warrior for God, you must surround yourself with other dangerous men of God that are mission oriented. By doing this, you are joining forces with valuable allies in the spiritual realm. In so doing, you will also be afforded with an opportunity to fight for them as they fight for you. Remember, you keep your sword sharp only by using it.

But who are dangerous men of God? Dangerous men of God are warriors that take everyday for what it is, a gift from God that must be fought for. They spend their time and energy getting to know God better (talking to Him), learning to walk in the paths he lays before them (they listen to him), and taking back what the Enemy has laid claim to (engages in spiritual warfare). Dangerous men of God can always be counted on and trusted. Most of all, dangerous men of God have your back and will gladly teach you what they know so that you may draw strength from them.

The biggest obstacle you will encounter when you go looking for dangerous men of God is that they are hard to find. Today's Church is just not readily producing them because of the lack of the right kind of Men's Ministries. In fact, most men of the Church are only learning how to be "Church Members", and little more, by watching the guys around them. Because of this fact, I have always wanted to have a t-shirt made that says "Everything I learned about being a Christian man, I learned from the older guys at my Church". In a way, that is true for all men. When we become a Christian, we look around and take notice of how the other guys that we view as more mature are doing things and try to pattern them. The only problem with this fact is that we have talked about how the Christian men of today are going about things wrong. The logical path of this tells us that we are doing things wrong too. Good grief! What do we do now?

Since God designed us for battle, there is a dangerous man of God lurking within each and every one of us. The problem is, this personality must be drawn out into the open and allowed to grow. But how? The best way I can explain it is by telling the story of my band of warriors.

A few years ago, I was the Men's Ministry Leader, a Church Council Member, and a Youth Counselor. On top of that, my wife and I had a new born baby to take care of. When you throw two sixty-hour a week jobs in the mix, you can see that we had a lot on our plates. I didn't have time to do one thing well, let alone all three for the Church. But luckily, some changes occurred in our leadership structure which allowed me to concentrate on the Men's Ministry only. The only problem was, we weren't getting anywhere. I was following the patterns of how the Men's Ministry had always been run and felt like I was swimming in a stagnate pond. We were getting together once per month and eating, and that was it. Nothing else outside of this was going on in the lives of the men of my Church. It was then that God gave me a burning desire for building relationships and growing the ministry from the inside out.

Since small group ministry was going well at our Church, my Pastor and I researched and selected a "men-only" small group. We decided to kick it off after a Thursday night chili supper. What a disaster, by the time everyone had eaten then made it into the sanctuary, it was already 7:30 PM and the men were only looking forward to getting home. This first attempt was a total failure because, there again, I followed the old pattern of doing things.

It was right after this first botched attempt that I began praying for God to give me direction. Up to this point, it was obvious that I had been doing things my way and not His way. The Lord led me to offer the small group as a class on Wednesday nights at the Church and He even sent me a helper in the form of my friend Mark. Mark had recently gone through this same small group study, and being a true Bible scholar, he was chomping at the bit to bring a new message to the men.

We launched the class and had twelve men show up the first night. The next Wednesday, twenty four men showed up! Obviously, the men of my Church were hungry and this offering had really struck a chord with them. The class went on for ten weeks and in that time our numbers dwindled some due to work conflicts, vacations, etc. When it was all said and done, this simple class finished up with ten men that had formed a tight bond with each other. We had grown together and felt as though we new each other intimately because each man had opened up their hearts to one another and even discussed things that most had never talked about to anyone other than maybe their spouse. My prayers were being answered: A core group of men had finally come together, got to know each others hearts, and built strong relationships with each other.

Now that we new each other's hearts, we knew more of what our individual needs were. When we finished the study, we continued to meet with each other on the same night each week. The only difference this time was that we transitioned from learning each others heart to going to war for each other.

I remember the first night we met after the study was completed. Our group of men traveled into the woods adjacent to the Church just because that's where we all felt like we needed to go. We were sitting in the woods talking about this and that, you know the usual "Ain't life great" stuff that guys are famous for, when my friend Randy asked us all a simple question. He simply asked each one of us, "What do you want?" He explained that as Jesus had done when he asked those he healed of their problems; he was asking each of us what was on our hearts, and what needs and desires we needed prayer for. Thinking back on that moment, Randy was simply marking out the battlefield and developing a strategy.

After everyone had answered to what the desire of their heart was, we went to prayer. That was the single most important moment of our Men's Ministry at my Church. At that moment, twelve brothers drew their swords and started fighting for each other like men. This was the defining moment that broke the mold of Men's Ministry for the future generations.

We still gather and pray for each other's needs. Although our men's ministry has grown larger and branched out into other bands of praying men, our initial core group still locks arms and fights for each other daily. This group of "Dangerous Men of God" helped me to see the battle for our souls as it is, all out bloody warfare.

As you can see, successful warrior culture must be built upon relationships with other men. Men have to really get to know each other before they will freely share what's in the deep recesses of their hearts. Once a man begins to pray for his fellow brothers and fight with and for them, a special kinship develops. As an old soldier myself, there is no stronger bond than between two soldiers that have served in the same foxhole together.

As we prayed and grew together, we learned that it took all of us (the whole team) to effectively fight against the Enemy's schemes and afflictions. It is so true that every man has his specific place in the battle that is unique to the gifts God has given him. A better way of saying this bluntly is: There is no one else on Earth that can fill in your spot on the front line. Your fellow soldiers need you and are weakened by your absence.

I have always been fascinated with the American Civil War. The thought of fighting with the tactics these men used frightens me to no end. These brave men stood within a stones throw of each other and fired volley after volley into each other's line. They did not hide from each other behind boulders or trees, they simply stood in formation firing and reloading their rifles, waiting to be struck down by an enemy bullet or incoming artillery. As the men in the front of the line fell dead, men behind them would fill in the vacancy. However, most of the time there was no one else to fill in and the line would simply collapse. If you fell over wounded, dead, or even if you deserted in the thick of battle, your comrades had to take up the slack and try to fill in for you. Each soldier was vital to victory and was not easily replaced. This is no different in a warrior culture of praying men because you cannot be replaced. The success of your comrades hinges on you and you alone. The Apostle Paul stressed this point when he said:

"So in Christ we who are many form one body, and each member belongs to all the others. We have different gifts according to the grace given us." (Romans 12:5-6)

You are special, you are needed, and most of all lives are at stake. There has never been a more desperate hour than the one that is upon us. Your sword is vital and you will become stronger as you fight alongside other warriors.

Fighting with and for other Christians will help to battle-harden you. We become battle hardened by being there in the action and refusing to back down. Battle hardened troops realize they are in a war that will not end until they have fought through the valley and over the mountain top, all the while spilling their own blood for the sake of their comrades. Remember, we don't fight an earthly battle with earthly weapons, our battle is in the supernatural and unseen world. We prepare by putting on the full armor of God, every hour, minute, and second of every day and then take up our swords and pray.

The first rule I learned upon reaching Army Basic Training was that a soldier never leaves anyone behind. When the man next to you falls, you pick him up and motivate him on. When I was in college I remember seeing the news footage of our fallen soldiers in Somalia as they were drug through the streets and mutilated by the enemy. I still carry these pictures in my mind and they are the most vile and disgusting images I have ever seen. Looking back, I wish I had never seen them in the first place.

However, these images only reinforce the need for Christian men to make a vow that they will never leave anyone behind.

When a Christian man succumbs to an attack of the Enemy and is beaten down, he is at a critical junction in his spiritual life because he can fight or give up. He is already weak from the battle and it is crucial that he enlist the services of other Christian men to lift him up and fight for him. These reinforcements can give him their strength and help him out of the darkness and into the light. I should know because I've been there. If it weren't for my warrior brothers fighting for me when I had reached my weak point, I would not be writing this book today.

When a man completely gives up fighting, you can be sure that he will be drug through the streets and mutilated by the Enemy. The Enemy will first attack his heart and attempt to isolate him from God, and maybe even tell him that God has abandoned him. It is our duty as warriors for God to check in with our spiritual brothers and look for signs of weakness and separation. If we sit back and watch them give up, we are the ones responsible for it because we both knew about it and we failed to react. A man left to go it alone is traveling down the road away from God. Every minute is critical and the clock is ticking away.

In addition to watching for signs of attacks against your brothers, warriors must also be willing to adapt to the changing landscape of battle. We must be dynamic because our Enemy sure is. Do you remember how Shaka Zulu revolutionized warfare and ultimately took over southern Africa? The key to his success was obviously his ability to recognize how his opponents fought and how he could adjust his tactics to reveal their weaknesses and ultimately gain victory. Shaka obviously viewed change as a good thing and allowed his army to evolve with the changing culture of warfare in his area.

At first, Shaka took everyone by surprise and conquered them simply by doing something new. When other tribes began to catch on to his fighting style and tried to emulate him, he evolved again with other tactics that could overcome his enemies. He was staying one step ahead, at all times. This is why he never tasted defeat in his lifetime. Even when the Europeans came bearing rifles, he learned that he could overpower them with numbers because he learned that their primary weakness was that they had to stop fighting and reload after every volley was fired.

After Shaka died, the Zulu people lost their vision and ability to change. Although Shaka's subsequent commanders were well versed in his tactics, they lacked the capability to change and evolve their methods of battle. When this happened, the once mighty Zulus were ultimately defeated. A warrior culture of Christians is no different. It must be dynamic and willing to change in order to survive.

All Christian warriors must stay on top of this constantly changing battlefield and at the tip of the sword. They must also be sensitive to the needs of the men around them and ever ready to snatch victory from the enemy while simultaneously watching the horizon for his next wave of attacks. Warriors in the army of God must evolve as they grow in spirit and in power. Not only for the advancement of the Kingdom, but because there is a powerful Enemy that is able to change his tactics mid-stream and will hit you in new ways you have never seen.

I've heard it said all my life to expect the unexpected from time to time. When it comes to attacks from the Enemy, we must "Expect the unexpected, Always!". The Enemy is always watching and patiently waiting for the right moment to pounce. He loves coming at us in new ways that we may have never expected, especially when we think we've gotten a leg up on him. One of my rules of thumb is this: When the thought crosses my mind that things are going well in my life and everything is peachy, I immediately armor-up and get prepared because I know it's coming.

When we prepare, we must know that Satan is the craftiest, wisest, and most ruthless master of guerrilla warfare on Earth. But what is guerrilla warfare anyway? *Guerrilla* comes from the Spanish term that means "little war". Since we equate little as meaning less in value, Satan wants us to believe that he is not there and his game plan of attack is to use a series of little wars meant to break us down over time. Satan uses these types of small attacks to destabilize our spiritual lives and confuse us. What a Warrior Culture must be able to do, is identify the small, guerrilla attacks and not pass them off with "Oh well, that's life!".

When I was a kid, my knees were constantly scabbed up due to bicycle wrecks. I grew up in the days of daredevils like Evil Kenevil that risked their lives doing crazy stunts. Well, I guess some of this rubbed off on me too. I wanted to be like these guys I saw on TV, so my best friend Chris and I would use our bikes to emulate them the best we could. Inevitably, the pavement normally won and I was left with bloody knees. In fact, like many of you, my knees still bear the marks left from this scaring over of my skin. The neat thing about scars is that they are generated during the healing process. When your skin is cut or scraped, new tissue immediately begins to grow in order to replace what has been removed. When the new wounded area has been covered in new skin, you are left with scar tissue. If it weren't for scarring, all of our wounds would remain open allowing a superhighway for infection to enter our body.

When we fight spiritual battles, you can expect to receive your fair share of spiritual battle scars. Scars received in the spiritual realm mirror the physical scars and are created during the healing process. Our scars also serve as a reminder of battles fought and the price that you personally paid and they may itch every now and then as a reminder of a past battle that we overcame. Above all, scars are a sure sign to the Enemy that you are a warrior and though he may wound you, your Savior has already overcome him.

As I said, scars are the outcome of the healing process. What I failed to tell you was that to be healed, you first have to be wounded. The wounds you can receive during seasons of spiritual warfare are very real and often times extremely painful. We receive these wounds from either the Enemy, by your own hand, or from other Christians.

I've talked a lot in this book about how the Enemy attacks. Sometimes he uses covert tactics like telling you he's not really there or small guerrilla attacks that may go unseen or at least not related to a spiritual attack. While other times he resorts to full frontal assaults such as sicknesses and oppression that he levels against us. The object of every attack, both large and small, is to weaken you and to distance you from God. When we became a child of God, we went from darkness (where Satan had a claim on our life) to light. Satan is not happy that he lost you and he will stop at nothing to get you back. If you haven't been told this already, prepare to be attacked. If you are not under attack, either you are not where you should be spiritually or you choose to believe the Enemy is not there. Although it is no fun to be under attack, we should rejoice in those times because the Enemy would not attack us unless we were doing something right.

Wounds not only come from the Enemy; they can also be self inflicted. Have you ever had somebody tell you something like, "Hey man, your arm is bleeding."? Most times you never even knew you had cut yourself, but there it is, flowing bright red. The same can be true for self inflicted spiritual wounds. In fact, the worst of these are the ones that we walk around carrying, clueless to the fact that we are bleeding. The worst thing about them is that if we do not notice them soon enough, we may bleed to death.

I mentioned in a previous chapter how one of my Brothers was blunt with me about how I was isolated from the pack and had been picked off. He noticed that I was bleeding from a gapping wound that only Jesus could heal. If not for him, I would have surely bled to death. This is a primary characteristic of a warrior. He is in tune with the hearts of the men around him. The warrior knows what his brothers in arms are capable of and he is sure to watch out for them and let them know where they are bleeding.

We've established that we can wound ourselves, but can we be wounded by fratricide (friendly fire) at the hands of other Christians? Yes indeed we can and these wounds are often the hardest ones to heal. The Department of Defense reported that 35 out of the 146 soldiers killed in Operation Desert Storm can be attributed to fratricide. It saddens me to think that 24% of our soldiers were killed by the hands of other Americans. Though it is an unfortunate statistic, it is a very real part of warfare. My good friend Craig was in the heat of battle with the 24th Mechanized Infantry and he told me, "It was total chaos. You didn't have time to think, you just aimed and fired as quick as you could at whatever was moving that looked like an enemy target." What my friend described is a very real condition that humans experience that is referred to as the "Fog of War". This condition directly influences the fratricide rate of every battle because when the fog sets in, mistakes occur more often, and unfortunately, people are accidentally killed.

Fratricide claimed many lives in the Iraqi desert due to the thick Fog of War and it is claiming lives today on the spiritual battlefield. Often times, the Enemy will choose to use other Christians against us. When we are hurt by another Christian, we see it as a betrayal of the faith. What we sometimes fail to realize is that Christians are people too and are bound to make mistakes. Remember, we're not perfect, just forgiven. Christians let each other down all the time and when they do, the Enemy is waiting to spring the trap. Most times he will tell you things like, "He did that on purpose", or "He thinks he is better than you", or the one I hear the most, "You might as well never talk to them again.".

There is only one way to heal the wounds of fratricide and it is called confrontation followed by forgiveness. Jesus spelled it out for us in Mathew 18 when he told the disciples:

> "If your brother sins against you, go and show him his fault, just between the two of you. If he listens to you, you have won your brother over. But if he will not listen, take one or two others along, so that every matter may be established by the testimony of two or three witnesses. If he refuses to listen to them, tell it to the Church; and if he refuses to listen even to the Church, treat him as you would a pagan or a tax collector." (Matt 18:15-17)

He's pretty straight forward here when he says if a brother (another Christian) **sins** against you, you must go to them and tell them man-to-man what they have done. This is the first step towards recovery of your relationship. But, Jesus knew how hard-headed we could be so he followed this up by telling us that if the person you go to will not listen to you then you need to get a few others and confront them again. Maybe a few witnesses will help you convince them. But then he really turns up the heat by telling us that if the person still refuses to listen then you take them before the Church! I think I missed something along the way because I have never seen this happen before.

I'm sure that most of you have never seen this happen either. Oh sure, I've heard rumors but never witnessed it. Jesus made it clear to us that if one of our brothers has wounded us in any way, we are to quickly go to them and talk about it. The Enemy and the flesh are both cowards and want us to stick our heads in the sand and ignore the problem hoping it will go away. The scary thing about this "ostrich" approach is that it will ultimately lead to our demise. We all know that forgiveness can be difficult at times because pride tends to get in the way. However, we are not told it is a nice thing to do, we are told by God himself that we <u>must</u> do it. And if you are wondering how many times you must follow this plan of forgiveness:

"Then Peter came to Jesus and asked, "Lord, how many times shall I forgive my brother when he sins against me? Up to seven times?" Jesus answered, "I tell you, not seven times, but seventy-seven times" (Matt 18:21-22)

490 (seventy times seven) is not a cumulative running total for only you in your life but it is a number specifically assigned to every person on Earth. Even though you are given a specific "Religious" boundary to follow, spiritually you should never keep score because Jesus didn't. Think about it this way, you are mandated (in the red letters) to forgive everyone, all the time. But what is spiritual forgiveness? Spiritual forgiveness is the ability to love someone no matter what they may have done to you because you have the knowledge that God loves them just as much as He loves you. If you have any doubts about this train of thought, just remember His example: He was stripped, beaten, flogged, ridiculed, spat upon, and nailed to a cross. Even though all of these things had been done to him, He forgave the ones that crucified him! Spiritual forgiveness is the catalyst that begins the healing process.

I love war movies, especially the ones in black and white. In all the great battlefield scenes whenever a soldier is shot, the first thing they do is scream "MEDIC!" Actually, this is pretty much how we do it in the military today. When the word "Medic" is called out, it means someone is wounded and is in need of immediate medical attention. The Medic must brave the crossfire and explosions of the battlefield and race to the casualty so that they may render medical care. On the spiritual battlefield, every warrior must often fill in as a medic. Up to this point all we have talked an awful lot about fighting and a little about healing. But one very important component of the Warrior Culture that must be established is a hospital for the wounded.

Every battle weary Christian must be nurtured back to health by other warriors. As I wrote earlier, the Enemy loves to attack us when we are weak, tired, and isolated. His tactic to kick us while we are down is one of the favorite arrows in his quiver. It is up to us to be the hospital for the battlefield wounded. When we are inundated with constant spiritual attacks, we must regain our strength by drawing it from other Christians. We draw this strength by receiving their prayers and encouragement.

One of my fellow warriors called me the other day and asked me for his help. He told me he had been under a constant barrage from the Enemy and he needed a break. We started praying that the spirit coming against him would be identified and banished in the name of Jesus. We actually were very vocal and demanding for him to leave. It was then that my brother in Christ started regaining his strength. I was a bit battle tired afterward but was happy that I could give some of my strength to him. It is when we place our friends in the mercy seat of Christ that the power of God can flow through them. As a follow up, I made sure to stay in contact with him for a few days offering some words of encouragement, but also to make sure he was recovering and not slipping into a pitfall.

Nursing your brothers back to health by fighting for them and standing in for them is what a Warrior Culture is all about. It's not a social club or an accountability group, it is about fighting tooth and nail for those you love. The reward that awaits you is seeing your brothers around you restored in Christ and overcoming the Enemy.

A valuable thing to remember is that you should never get too comfortable with victory. The war you were born into will not end anytime soon. Remember Joab and Abishai and how their dependence on each other led to victory for King David? Do you know what happened next? In the very next chapter, David was so happy with his success that he got "fat and sassy" and stayed home from the war. That's when he looked down from his roof and saw Bathsheba naked and he lusted for her through his fleshly eyes. David dropped his guard for one minute and the next thing you know he had made her pregnant and sent her husband off to war in hopes he would die in order to cover up for his mistake. This story of David is a good reminder to all Christians that although you may achieve some victories and overcome some obstacles, you still have to stay on alert. The Enemy will always try to sneak one in under your radar using his good buddy flesh just when we think we've beaten him.

Chapter 7
Lead from the Front

The Hundred Years War was a series of brutal clashes of English and French forces between the years 1337 and 1445. I never understood why it was called the "Hundred" when it lasted for 108 years. I guess it's just easier to round down isn't it? Anyway, the primary goal of the English campaign was to take back land in Normandy that they felt was rightfully theirs. The majority of the battles fought in this long and weary conflict were more or less fruitless for either side and resulted in many lives lost and little ground taken.

However, one leader was immortalized for his bravery in this war by William Shakespeare in his play Henry V. In the Fall of 1415, the English forces lead by Henry V had fought hard but lost many men due not only to battle but also to disease and malnutrition. They were battle weary and dysentery-ridden during a retreat to the port of Calais where they hoped to return to England. Unbeknownst to them, a superior French force raced ahead of them and blocked their path at an area known as Agincourt. The English force of an estimated 5,900 troops faced very little hope of victory against the French that numbered them by approximately 30,000 men.

It was October 25th, Saint Crispian's Day to the English, when they awoke to a muddy battlefield due to torrential rains from the previous night. The men were wet, cold and tired as they formed up for battle. Meanwhile, the French forces must have felt far superior to the English because they fielded a more advanced army of horse cavalry supported by foot soldiers wearing heavy armor.

What happened next is up for debate. Historical accounts of the battle suggest that Henry V roused his men with a stirring speech from horseback in which he told them to fight hard because their only option was death. However, Shakespeare's version is much more inspiring when he penned King Henry as saying the following speech to his ragtag band of warriors:

This day is called the feast of Crispian:
He that outlives this day, and comes
safe home,
Will stand a tip-toe when the day is named,
And rouse him at the name of Crispian.
He that shall live this day, and see old age,
Will yearly on the vigil feast his neighbors,
And say, "Tomorrow is Saint Crispian":
Then will he strip his sleeve

and show his scars.
And say, "These wounds I had on
Crispin's Day."
Old men forget: Yet all shall be forgot,
But he'll remember with advantages
What feats he did that day: then
shall our names,
Familiar in his mouth as household words
Harry the King, Bedford, Exeter, Warwick
and Talbot, Salisbury and Gloucester,
Be in their flowing cups
freshly remembered.
This story shall the good man teach his son;
And Crispin Crispian shall ne'er go by,
From this day to the ending of the world,
But we in it shall be remembered;
We few, we happy few, we band of brothers;
For he today that sheds his blood with me
Shall be my brother; be he ne'er so vile,
This day shall gentle his condition:
And gentlemen in England now a-bed
Shall think themselves accursed they were
not here,
And hold their manhood's cheap
whiles any speaks
That fought with us upon
Saint Crispin's Day.

What happened next is known as one of the
greatest reversals of fortune in military history. When
the French attacked, they became bogged down in the
heavy mud and some even drowned due to the weight

of their armor. Also, the French cavalry was neutralized because the horses sank in the field. Because the English wore little or no armor, they were more nimble and did not fall casualty to the quagmire of the battlefield. The French were in essence rendered helpless and the English fell upon them with knives, hatchets, and mallets and slaughtered them. When the battle was over, the body count was between 12,000 and 18,000 French dead or wounded while as best can be determined only around 200 English soldiers met the same fate.

As the English proved at Agincourt, It is never too late to snatch victory from the jaws of defeat. The greatest thing about all of this is that it can all start with you! God designed you to be a leader like Henry V whether you choose to believe it or not. God is the ultimate leader and He created you in His image and wrote the qualities of leadership on your heart. At your disposal is His limitless source of power that will help you uncover them. Believe me, leadership ability is in you, waiting patiently in the deep recesses of your heart, struggling to be unleashed for His glory. That is why the Enemy seeks to discourage you; he is frightened by what will happen when you are set free.

When we attempt to step up in Christian leadership, the Enemy likes to strike quickly with the spirits of discouragement. He knows if he can discourage us and cause us to lose site of our vision, he wins. I have had this happen in my own life and can tell you from experience, it can put you in a position that you don't ever want to be by making you question your own salvation.

About a year after I rededicated my life to the Lord, I was selected to by the congregation to be a member of my Church's Leadership Council. When elected by the body, I was humbled that I had been chosen to represent our members. Although I had experience in business and military leadership, this was my first experience in Church leadership. I was excited about this new position because I knew that I could finally use my gift of administration to glorify God. I jumped right in with both feet and attended the monthly Board meetings where we discussed, tabled, and enacted the programs and policies that the Church would operate under. After a few meetings, I had become very comfortable helping steer the "Church boat". Since I had management experience I couldn't wait to take my knowledge and talents and use them at my favorite place in the world, my Church. And even better, this time I would be in God's house with God's people. How wonderful it would be to lead in an environment where God was put first in everything along with his good and perfect will. Since I felt I was finally in the perfect place, I settled in and got comfortable.

Of course, as soon as we become comfortable,
the Enemy will attack.

The attacks began subtly at first. For example, in one meeting, a discussion broke out in which the council was divided on an issue. I was shocked! I thought that if we are all of one spirit, all decisions would be unanimous because after all, we are all Christians and we hold to the same basic belief structure. I couldn't believe that Christians could disagree and even worse, I began to doubt the spirituality of the other leaders on the Board. Where could those ideas and feelings have come from? Looking back, it is obvious that the Enemy was there whispering to me that Christians shouldn't disagree because they are supposed to be perfect.

I agreed with the Enemy's lies because I had grown up thinking the Church was a "perfect world" where everybody got along and Christians lived in perfect harmony. Well, if you believe this way, I hate to break it to you but you are wrong. I soon found out that the Church is not without its share of problems. Think about it, any organization that is run by man cannot be perfect simply due to our fallen nature. Although God is the head of every Church, he entrusts man to facilitate it. And, if our track record shows anything, it is that we have proved over and over that we are creatures of disagreement, arguments, and fall-outs. If you need proof of this, just open up the phone book and look at how many different Christian denominations reside in your town.

For the next year, the Enemy would use every negative thing that I heard about the Church to convince me that both the Church and myself were not good enough for God. I bought into his lie that the Church should never have internal conflicts or any kind of uncomfortable matters happening within it's doors. After all, Church is not supposed to be of the world where real problems and conflicts occur. Church is supposed to be a holy city on a hill that shows the glory of the Lord.

It was after a year of repeated condemnation by the Enemy that I cut a deal and let him win. I let the Enemy convince me that I was not cut out for being a Council member at my own Church. The problem I now faced was that I couldn't bring myself to resign because my pride worried about what others would think. So, I did the cowardly thing and made every excuse in the world to skip out on the meetings. I was at my wits end and that is precisely when God took over!

One day, I was praying and asking God to show me what was wrong and to step in and fix the problems in the Church. I have to admit that my selfish desire was to want all the problems solved on my time and not his. So guess what, he didn't fix them on my time and he let them build up to a climax! Things got worse and worse (in my eyes) to a point where I couldn't stand even going to Church and wanted to start going to another place of worship. That was when he opened my eyes and helped me identify that I was under attack. At that moment, I realized I had to start fighting it off. So, I started fighting the Enemy's attacks and listening to God. I also prayed that God would help me overcome this distrust and dislike for the Church that I had developed. I knew that if I didn't overcome this, I would never be able to fulfill the role I had been selected to play as a Council member.

About two months later, God came through in his own way and on his time. Out of the blue, our Church voted overwhelmingly to change the leadership structure. The new structure would be formed by combining the Board of Trustees and Church Leadership Council that I was on, into a single Board of Elders. The first set of Elders would be selected by the current Trustees and Council members and brought before the Church for a final vote. At first I was worried because I really didn't want to be an Elder due to all of the warfare I had gone through during my time on the Council.

When the Trustees and Council met as a joint body to select the first group of eleven Elders I was there and to be honest, I was scared to death that I would be selected. When the Pastor read through his list of potential selections, I was relieved to see that my name was not on it. This was a great relief because I was afraid I would be selected and that my heart wouldn't be in it. In other words, I feared letting down my Church and ultimately God.

We went around the room for about an hour prayerfully adding and also eliminating people from the list. After a while, you guessed it, I was added to the list. My heart sank in my chest and the fear returned. I thought to myself, "What am I going to do now?" That's when God showed up! The Pastor announced, "Is there anyone here that does not want to be considered as an Elder?" As if God had shouted into my ear to raise my hand, I immediately stuck my hand up high so that I could be scratched from the list. Once it was held high in the air, I felt somewhat embarrassed so I closed my eyes. When I opened them, I realized that I was not alone and there were a few others that had joined me. It was at that moment that I felt the weight of all the bad things I had been carrying around concerning my Church lifted from my shoulders. God was beginning to restore me.

Although I had peace, the Enemy quickly chimed in and whispered a constant barrage of lies to me to tear me down. He told me:

"You've really let the Pastor down this time."

And

"You'll never be selected for anything again."

And

"Some Christian servant you are!"

After a few days of this onslaught and praying against his attacks, God told my heart that He loved me and that I really do matter to Him. This was a very real and very tough battle that I had to fight my way through. Today I am stronger and I still have the same peace that God gave me. Also, God equipped me with a wealth of knowledge during that season that I hope to use if one day if I am selected to be an Elder.

In this book, I have tried to help men that are seeking to start and grow a vital group of warriors to fight with and draw strength from. As you can see from the previous story, I am no expert on Church politics but I have been enlightened to them greatly. The best way to put this to you is that politics exist everywhere and you will be opposed from time to time. And if that were not enough, the Enemy is the greatest politician that ever lived and he knows exactly what spin to put on things that will push your buttons every time.

The reason I am telling you this is to prepare you for the opposition you will face in Men's Ministry. As I've said before, the Enemy fears the idea of men locking arms and fighting against him in a united front. He will go to great lengths to oppose you and he will use whatever methods and people that he can to carry out his work. The question is not "Will he?" but "When will he?" The good thing about this opposition is that it gives you the opportunity to hone your leadership skills and ultimately grow stronger from it.

Leading others requires not only commitment and devotion but it also requires you to lead a life that others admire. Everyone that is a leader is under the microscope. It doesn't matter if you are a Sunday School teacher or the President of the United States, everywhere you go people will be watching you and taking down mental notes about how you act and react to real world situations. Sadly, most of time it is the flesh that is watching, hoping, and waiting for you to slip up so it can say "Ah-Ha, I told you so!". You must understand that as a leader, you will slip up and you will make mistakes. Also, there will always be critics standing in the wings waiting to tear you down. This is the battle the leader fights on a daily basis and it is staged in the pits of hell. The Enemy and the flesh work hand in hand through others, even Christians, to wage this war. It is real and it is coming, but now that you are in the know, you are better prepared to fight back.

Since leaders must plan on a never ending battle, they must have the strength and stamina of a boxer. Professional boxers dedicate their life to training in an attempt to be one step ahead of their opponent at all times. A boxer's training regime is highly specialized and concentrates on strength, stamina, and agility. Boxers build strength through a weight lifting program that focuses not only on the arms for punching strength but also on building up the legs. In fact, the legs are the building blocks of the boxer and without them a boxer will not have the stability they need when in the ring. The boxer spends hours building up the hip and leg muscles that act as the columns that hold his body while in the ring.

Strategy is also vital in the ring. The boxer must be able to adapt to his opponents style and continually adjust his fighting methods not only to protect himself from the barrage but also to exploit weaknesses. When a weakness is identified, it must be "keyed in on" and continually attacked. This is the key to victory; wearing down the opponent by exploiting one weak spot over and over.

The boxer must also be aware at all times of the mechanics of his fighting. He must stand in such a way as to protect him from strikes but must have the ability to strike out at will. There are many different techniques to use during the boxing match including the bob and weave, the parry, and the slip. But by far, the most important part of a boxer's technique is his punch. The punch may be in the form of a jab, cross, uppercut, or hook. All are effective when executed with power. Power is developed through the aforementioned weight training but it is perfected in the technique. Punches are an offensive weapon, but may also be used for defending the body from attack.

We've established the fact that the Enemy seeks to destroy any ministry that's mission is to unify men and help them come alive. As a leader of a Men's Ministry you must become a boxer and be in constant training. The Enemy will come after you and you had better be on your toes, ready to defend yourself from his attacks and punch back using the sword of the spirit. Remember, with the power of Christ in you, you have the power to overcome anything he may dish out. It is up to you to be armored up for that battle so that when it comes, you will have strong legs under you, your fighting stance set, and your punching technique perfected.

In addition to being a fighter, a leader must also be a coach. At the heart of every team is their center that is known as the Coach. Coaches spend their time crafting, encouraging, training, and directing their players. The Coach is the Captain of the ship and is sometimes even referred to as the "Skipper", especially in baseball. A lot is required of a Coach that many take for granted. The Coach must know their players inside and out and must develop a "sixth sense" that gives them the ability to know what is going on inside the mind of their athletes.

When we watch a game on television, we see the players executing plays and we may even see the Coach on the sidelines, but we never see what is really going on behind the scenes. When you step over the line and dedicate yourself to working with men in order to establish a warrior culture, you must be in tune with what's really going on in their lives. As I said earlier, men do not like to talk about their problems because it makes them feel weak. This part of a man, his private world the public doesn't see, is what is most important to him and will affect his relationship with God and others more than anything else. For example, maybe one of your players came to you just before the game and told you that his mother just died. Or, maybe two players got in a fight with each other in the locker room before warm ups. These unseen things are what can kill a team and it is up to the Coach to fix them. Running plays and performing on the field is the easy part, it's the behind the scenes aspect of coaching that is the greatest challenge.

Leading men at Church is a lot like coaching a team of athletes. All men put on their "game face" in order to hide the inner weaknesses they are carrying. They use these masks at Church, work, and other functions as they run the plays they know by heart. But what about the behind the scenes aspect of Church going men? Remember Stan and Dave? You saw the outer conversation and I clued you in to a little about what was going on but let's go a little deeper. Stan has been out of work and has no hope of finding a job. It's tearing his family apart and he is considering relocating them against their will. On top of that, his finances are in such shambles that he lays awake at night worrying about how he will feed his family. But Dave is no better off. He has a thriving business but his partner is about to go down for tax evasion and he is sure he will be drug into it and could possibly lose everything in the process. Would you have ever guessed this if you would have been standing there when they had their fake little conversation?

Therein lies the problem, men desperately need other men to call their bluff. I mentioned before how my friend Randy called my bluff after I had fallen away from our warrior group. If not for his spirit-led actions, I know I would not be where I am today both spiritually and physically. It is because of pride and what my Grand-paw referred to as "hard-headedness" that the majority of men take offense to any form of criticism leveled at them. To become a warrior for the Kingdom, you must grow a thicker layer of skin that will help you take criticism from others.

Just as Randy did for me, you must also be open and honest with other men so that you can lovingly criticize them when you feel prompted to do so. But be on your guard before you speak out, the Enemy loves to lurk in criticism. You must always test the spirits through prayer to make sure they are from God and not from the Enemy or the flesh. The Enemy loves to tear down relationships by using condemnation. You will know if the ideas are from the Enemy if they condemn your brother rather than try to help him.

Every leader must also be willing to sacrifice for the good of the team. We have already been given the perfect example of sacrifice in what Jesus did for us on the cross. A leader must be able to always put his men ahead of his own desires and agendas. The men that you lead are your responsibility and your agenda is only details. When we put others ahead of our own desires we not only sacrifice for them, but we also display the servant heart that Christ modeled for us.

Sacrifice may also involve giving up the comfort zone you enjoy in order to reach out to men that need you. It is human nature to enjoy the security in your comfort zone, but this is anything but Christ like. Think about it, Jesus stepped out of the most comfortable existence that there is and ever will be when he left heaven. He came to this Earth, wrapped himself in human flesh, and made his way through this dark and dirty world. There is no possible way for us to even come close to imitating his act of sacrifice but we must use it as a model to live by. Living a life of sacrifice involves removing fear from your life as you step out into the unknown. This is the only way you will ever be able to reach those that the Enemy has already claimed.

Now, many people think that to be an effective leader, you must portray a certain image. This is a worldly idea spurred on by today's business climate. Corporate America revolves around having a perfect, false image that is used to impress others. This false image may include where your parking place is at the office, who you have lunch with, where your suit was made, or even where you went on vacation last year. Obviously, if you've paid any attention at all, you will realize that this is a smokescreen the Enemy likes to hide behind known as vanity. In Christ, these things have no meaning and will not make you any more spiritual than the homeless living on the street. So in other words, it doesn't matter what you look like, how you dress, or what you drive, leadership demands only humbleness and a passion for the burden God has given you. If you have a passion for what you are doing, God will equip and guide you along the path that he has laid out for you.

To be an effective leader of men, you have to "Lead from the front". The great warrior Audie Murphy is credited with that saying and it is has been used by countless public speakers to encourage and fire up potential leaders. Leading from the front is very pertinent to leading men of the Church also. Not only because it is a great quality of a leader but also because of the testimony of Murphy's life of persistence.

Audie Murphy was born to poor Texas share-croppers in Texas. When Pearl Harbor was bombed, Murphy tried to join the Army but was rejected because he was too young. When he turned 18 he enlisted and was sent off to basic training. His goal was to become a combat infantryman but due to his frail appearance, he was threatened with a transfer to cook school. He persisted in his training and proved that he was strong enough for the infantry and after the invasion of Europe, he found himself at the front lines. This man with humble roots and a burning desire to fight went on to be the most decorated soldier of all time. Murphy's bravery on the battlefield has never since, nor probably ever will be eclipsed.

Like Murphy, you must take the initiative and get started on your own. If you haven't caught on by now, I'll spell it out for you: You cannot rely on anyone but yourself to get it started. But before we get into the guts of starting up, let's make sure we keep our focus clear:

> Men's Ministry is about building relationships and bonds between men, not about starting more Church programs.

You have to be all about growing men together as a united warrior front. You are not starting a social club, you are enlisting soldiers into an army of dangerous men. These men are vital to the world because there is an Enemy that, "Comes ONLY to steal, kill, and destroy" (John 10:10). The reality is that lives, families, and Churches are at stake.

Chapter 8
I Read Your Book, Now What?

I've talked about key things that will help jump start your ministry; Now, let's talk about what you should avoid. First things first, don't run out and organize a pancake breakfast or start another boring bible study. Yuck! That is where the Church has messed up for years. Men are not looking for another way to give up their time, they are looking for acceptance and a place to belong. That is why your first stop must be at the Pastor's office. If you are planning on starting or even just upgrading the Men's Ministry in your Church, you must have 100% of your Pastor's support. What I have talked about in this book is most likely a break from the norm for most Churches. Going forward, it is vital to have the endorsed, seal of approval from the leader of your Church. This is also a great opportunity for you and the Pastor to pray together and draw strength from on another.

Don't be surprised if the Pastor is a bit over-whelmed by the barrage of ideas you present to him. The fact is, the majority of Pastors are not use to men coming to them with ideas for ministries; they are accustomed to women doing this. So if you meet resistance, assure your Pastor that it is in his best interest to help you begin to unite the men of his Church and transform them into warriors for the Kingdom.

One way to begin transforming men into warriors is by the formation of a Pastoral Prayer Team. This is a team comprised of only men with the sole respon-sibility of fighting on their knees for the Pastor/s. Members of this group should be prayerfully consid-ered by the Pastor and yourself. I have personally witnessed the fruit that a group of prayer warriors that pray for their Pastor prior to and during the services can bring. There is not a doubt in my mind that the Enemy is extremely interested in attacking those called of God to Pastor His people. The Pastor needs you to have his back because the damage done when a Church leader is picked off is most of the time irreparable. By forming a squad of warriors that pray for the Pastor, you are taking a great step in making an offensive strike at the Enemy.

The strength of a group of men praying together can best be described in the fourth chapter of Acts. In this chapter, the followers of Christ had lifted up their prayers and petitions to God in one heart. So, what did He do? He sent his Spirit to shake, rattle, and roll the whole place where they were praying! This event is well known as Pentecost and it set the standard for how the power of God can be physically manifest in this world if we will ask him for it.

The power of God is not only manifested in the petitions that are lifted up to Him, but it is also in the bonds that are formed between the praying men. This is because the praying man is revealing his true heart when he prays aloud. Those that hear him are seeing into his unveiled and naked heart. This vulnerability is what builds trust between men and ultimately leads to deeper relationships with one another.

For many years, the Church has produced exactly what it is set up to produce: nice little Christian guys. What the Church is in dire need of are warriors that are not afraid to fight like men, stand up for what is right, and awaken others to join into this culture. But why aren't our Churches automatically rolling out warrior men like Ford rolls out Mustangs? The answer to this can be found in the way Jesus has been portrayed and what we have been taught about masculinity.

To begin with, we have to look at what has gone on in the Church over the past two hundred years In the Victorian Era, Jesus was feminized and turned into a "Sweet Little Jesus" that hugged kids and loved everyone. Both of those aspects are true in a way, but these qualities of Jesus are the most commonly taught, especially to the children today. In fact, I thought Jesus grew up as a wimp that carried around a lamb on his shoulder. I was shocked the day I studied how he took a whip and used it on the money changers! But it wasn't just the money changers. Jesus was most known for questioning what the religious leaders of the time considered unquestionable. Every chance Jesus had to argue, fight, and defeat the self righteous, he took it. And guess what, he never lost a fight. He is the perfect model of a warrior that all men must strive to emulate in their lives.

Jesus not only had a mean streak, but I'm guessing he was pretty stout too. The boys of his time grew up learning the craft that their father used to provide for his family. It has been debated as to what Jesus' line of work was, but the most accepted occupation is that of a carpenter. Whether he was or not is irrelevant because we do know from the ancient texts that he worked with his hands. But to keep things simple, lets say he was a carpenter that built everything from homes to furniture. Now, think about what you would have to do if you wanted to build a simple chair using the technology and tools of that era. First you have to take an axe and chop down a tree. After the tree is fallen you would strip it by hand, hook it to a beast of burden, and drag it out of the woods. Then you have to use a hand saw to cut the tree into boards. After the boards are cut, you would have to work the wood until smooth. And then you would have to lay out the design, cut it and fasten the pieces together.

It's hard work for me to use power tools to build a birdhouse in my garage. I can't imagine building a chair starting with a tree trunk instead of wood from the local home improvement store. Because of this, I feel pretty safe saying that Jesus was very muscular and strong. This is such a departure from the pictures of the Victorian Jesus we so often see. You know the ones I'm talking about where he looks like an

Englishman and has blond hair, blue eyes, a pasty complexion, and a frail, almost feminine body. Let me ask you this, have you ever seen anyone from the Middle East that looks like this? Where is the dark hair and eyes and the olive complexion? What a lie we've bought into and believed.

When you think about it, not only Jesus but also the Church has become feminized. Look around on any given Sunday and you will find that women outnumber men in almost every congregation. Women also seem to be the most involved people in the Church. It is pretty obvious that more women are teaching Sunday School, planning events, and leading the worship of the Church than men. With women doing all of the teaching and planning, it is no wonder that the Church has taken on a feminine mystique.

But why? Is this because men are just lazy? To find the answer to this question, let us first take a peek into the business world. In Corporate America, men outnumber women in the leadership department. In fact, less than 3% of all Fortune 500 companies are run by women. So what happens after the work day is over and Church time rolls around? That's easy, the men for the most part try to blend in.

I've often said to myself, "Maybe men are sick and tired of leading in their jobs and like to be lead at Church so they can rest." I sure hope I am wrong on this one because this would mean that men are constantly denying the calling God has put on their lives. So, what could it be? I am starting to think that the real answer can be found in the great enemy of man that we spoke of earlier: Pride.

> *I have to believe that it is because of pride and the fear that it spawns that most men do not accept leadership positions at Church.*

When given an opportunity to teach a class, the average Christina man will fear they are not knowledgeable enough to teach God's word and they will look like a fool, or even worse teach the Word wrong. That is pride at its finest when it makes a man fear he will cast an image that he doesn't know what he is talking about and doesn't have what it takes.

Teaching a Bible class is a pretty large step in leadership, but how about a small one such as leading the congregation in a prayer? I know the first time I was asked to close a service with a word of prayer I practically choked to death. Was it because I didn't know how to pray? No, it was because I was afraid of sounding stupid and uneducated. The only place these feelings of inadequacy could have come from were from my own pride. I hope you have seen how the pride-generated fear of looking stupid in the eyes of others is one of the reasons men do not want to be more involved in Church leadership.

Another reason may be found in the fact that men are biologically wired differently than women. God set within every man the need to see things from the masculine perspective in order to really grasp concepts and ideas presented to them. One of the ways Church has attempted to solve this problem is by creating Men's Ministries where men can be men while they are there. God bless them for their work, but don't men need to be men everywhere in the Church? What good does it do to only practice manliness at Men's Ministry functions? This is an obvious problem in today's Church that tells men they can't be men in so called "Big Church". Instead, many Churches require men to sit nice and quiet and not question anything, just come to Church, tithe, and do what they're told to do. In essence, men are told to behave and better yet, "You'll have time for all the man stuff at your next men's meeting." I don't know about you but this makes me feel like I am right back in first grade!

Men need to be men, created in the image of their creator, at all times, not just when it is convenient for the Church and especially not only when it is scheduled. We can't help the way we were wired by God and we cannot change it. The bottom line is, we do not need to change because someone might be afraid we may mess up some image the Church is attempting to portray. This is just another way that religion gets in the way of spirituality.

I'm sure that by now you have heard the slogan, "Americans have been Churched to spiritual death." Well, it's true! For too many years we have been told to be there every Sunday and Wednesday and you better be dressed nice and have a smile on your face. If it wasn't said directly to you, it sure has been implied. And if that isn't enough, we've been repeatedly told to support every new program that is launched in the Church and tell everyone how great it is. On and on, week after week, the life was sucked out of me until one day I came to the realization that there is a vast divide between religion and spirituality. Religion is all about what you need to do to please the law of the Church while spirituality is about pleasing God through a relationship with Him. It's obvious to me that we do not need any more programs at our Churches that tell you what you must do to be a better Christian/Church Member. What we are dieing for in the Church is the need for relationships with each other and most of all with God. It is not until we walk with God, listen to him, and let him love us that we can be spiritual Christians that live from the proper motivations of our hearts.

So let me ask you this; is your relationship with God dependent upon how many times you go to Church? What about how much you tithe, how well you pray aloud, or how many times you've helped out at vacation bible school? Praise the Lord the answer to all of these is a resounding NO! But if the answer is no, then why has the Church tried to make us feel as though our salvation is dependent upon trivial matters such as these? Please don't think I am telling you to quit going to Church and stop volunteering, I am only trying to make the point that your relationship with God is a spiritual relationship not a religious one. In fact, to prove this point, Paul wrote to the Philippians:

> "Therefore, my dear friends, as you have always obeyed-not only in my presence, but now much more in my absence-continue to

work out your salvation with fear and trem-
bling, " (Ph 2:12)

Your salvation is in your hands to be worked
out by you while walking with God. There is no one
on Earth that can judge you. The politics of many
Churches have a way of building walls between
people that God detests. Don't let religiosity and
Church ever come between you and your creator. In
other words, stop playing Church!

For many years, I played Church because it was
something I thought I was expected to do. I had
completely missed out on the whole relationship
thing with my Savior and it was not until I began
walking daily with God that my life was transformed
and I felt truly saved. That's when the fog I had been
walking through lifted, and I started seeing things
clearly. And it's also when I heard God's calling on
my life to work with the guys around me to help them
see the bigger picture that I had been looking at.

I remember it like it was yesterday when I looked
around one Sunday morning and thought to myself,
"Am I the only guy here that knows about this?" and,
"Are there any other guys that are experiencing this
kind of spiritual growth by walking with God and
letting him equip me?" I found out there were a few
in my Church that were working on their own inti-
macy with God and I ran to them. We began seeking
God together through times of prayer and fasting and
we also started reaching out to other men around us
by offering "Men Only Gatherings". I'm not talking
about a bunch of guys eating pancakes and shooting

the bull, we started something more. We liked to refer to them as meetings of dangerous men coming together to fight. How do men fight you may ask? On their knees in prayer.

If I were to tell you, "Hey, meet me down at the park tonight around midnight, there's some dangerous men I want you to meet and hang out with for a while." What would you think? My first thought is rough looking characters in leather jackets and toting switch blades. But what if I told you these guys are all Christians. Now you are probably thinking, "What are Christians doing in a park at midnight? Aren't they afraid of getting hurt? What if the wrong people come along and want to fight?" Well, that's exactly why they are there, to fight. The "Wrong People" which are the Enemy and his goons, are there in the middle of the day and the night and wage war against all of us, all of the time.

But how do I get started building a band of warriors like this at my Church? Let me start off by saying that every situation and Church is different. There is no cut and dry method of building a Warrior Culture, only the ideas I've presented in this book. It is up to you to experiment with different methods but like I mentioned earlier, it all starts with Pastoral support. Once you have received Pastoral support and he knows exactly what you are all about, it's time to go to work.

I recommend that you start by prayerfully crafting a list of all the men that you deal with on a constant basis no matter how superficial your relationship may be with them (as in the Stan and Dave dialogue).

Next, go through your list and circle the names of the men that you feel you know the best. Maybe you have been to dinner with them or you just know them from your school days, these will be your first points of contact.

Making a list is the easy part, next comes the uncomfortable portion where you must step out of your comfort zone and talk to face to face with the men you have circled. The first rule of this step is, don't overwhelm them with all the dire facts you have learned. Use the K.I.S.S. approach (keep it simple stupid) to craft the words you want to use. It can be as simple as this:

> "Hey Dave, I wonder if you can help me out. I've been having a rough time lately with some guy stuff and I need your advice on something. Do you think you would have thirty minutes to talk this week? I could sure use your input."

Men are naturally hard-wired as problem solvers and should be more than eager to offer you advice. When Dave agrees to meet with you, set up a time convenient for both of you right then and there. Don't wait on him to get back with you because he probably will not. When you do sit down with him, first pray together and then explain how you want his help to build up the men of the Church. You don't have to be too technical, you are just trying to find a warrior that you can lock arms with and get the ball rolling. Some men will not want anything to do with it because they feel called to do other things. Don't be discouraged; count it a blessing that God is weeding out the ones that don't have their heart in the same place as you. Your initial goal is to establish the first leadership committee.

After you have four or five men that will help you, it's time for all of you to sit down and brainstorm. First things first, always begin with prayer and ask for God to lead your meeting, not you. The best way to open the first meeting is to start with a simple question like: "What do you think the shape of the men of this Church is today?" or "Where do we want to be as a ministry in ten years?" Each man will have an answer that is crucial to the direction your ministry will take. Use this time to throw out ideas to each other and most of all make sure to write them down.

One of the first institutions you should attempt to set up at this meeting is a Pastoral Prayer Team, with the Pastor's approval of course. I spoke about it before but didn't go into what it can do for the leadership team and the body of the Church. When your men pray together over the Pastor, bonds are made, the Pastor is given a renewed strength, and the Holy Spirit is released to war for him and the congregation. Also, when men come together to pray, they are introduced to fighting as a team. This team is the first step in building a Warrior Culture. If for some reason the Pastor does not want to be prayed over (I hope this is never the case), find another outlet for your team to pray. I cannot stress enough how it all starts with prayer. Whether you pray for the pastor, each other, the choir, or whatever you choose, praying together unites you as warriors.

The key to Men's Ministry growth is keeping the momentum going. Always be on the lookout with your spiritual eyes for opportunities to grow. There are many men's specific small group studies you can use to build relationships. I have found that when men come together and open up to one another, closeness develops that binds hearts to one another. One warning though, don't do a "Men's Bible Study" of a random book of the Bible. There is nothing revolutionary about this. Instead, do your homework. Research and find a study that appeals to the hearts of your men. In other words, find a Christian study that is about guy stuff and masculinity as it relates to God. They are out there and can be found by typing a few words into a search engine and clicking a mouse. But before you put stock in any particular study material, make sure to read over the author's statement of faith. Make sure you agree with it and by all means run it by your Pastor.

A little earlier, I told you to avoid the pancake breakfast at all costs. I should have explained that a little more by saying don't kick off your Men's Ministry with one. Instead, start with a leadership team, prayer groups, and small groups. These will start your group down the road to building the fundamental relationships that are vital to all men. There is nothing wrong with the guys getting together to eat and have fellowship, in fact God ordained it when Luke wrote:

"They devoted themselves to the apostles' teaching and to the fellowship, to the breaking of bread and to prayer." (Acts 2:42)

Table fellowship is one of the primary ways that Jesus showed his love for everyone. He loved to have them over and share a meal with them. During these meals, he acted out God's indiscriminate love for everyone in attendance regardless of what sins they were carrying. Jesus gave them his acceptance, peace, reconciliation, a sense of brotherhood, and most of all Joy! If you think about it, Salvation is Joy in God. Jesus imparted his saving grace to everyone He met back then and He's still doing it today. So don't think there is anything wrong with eating together. As Christ demonstrated, this is a perfect outlet for fellowship, as well as inviting the lost that may have never been around real men of God.

As men become more involved, expect some growing pains. You must be in tune with the changing battlefield conditions. You will be attacked, so you need to be putting on the armor of God every day and expecting the battle to come. The attack may come as a rumor you hear about people bad mouthing you, or you may be confronted by an angry wife. But whatever it is keep in mind that God is in control by referring to words of the Prophet Jeremiah that wrote:

"For I know the plans I have for you," declares the Lord, "Plans to prosper you and not to harm you, plans to give you hope and a future. Then you will call upon me and come and pray to me and I will listen to you. You will seek me and find me when you seek me with all of your heart. I will be found by you." declares the Lord, "and will bring you back from captivity." (Jer 29:11-14a)

It should be obvious to you by now that God has put a call on your life for Men's Ministry leadership or you wouldn't have made it this far in this book. What you must keep in mind is that when God gives you a calling, he never takes it back. You have been selected by Him for this mission in order to bring glory to His name. For reasons that are beyond our own mental capacity, God has selected you to build His kingdom by developing common men into Christian warriors. This is a huge task and requires talents that only God can give.

A Christian man is the most dangerous weapon for the Kingdom because God crafted every man in His warrior image. But it doesn't stop there because the Christian man carries in his heart, the Holy Spirit which is the most powerful being on earth. When a group of Christian warriors assembles together in the name of God and combines their swords, the power of God is unleashed to war against the Enemy. This is what the Enemy fears, warrior men of God that do battle against him, and raise up a warrior culture around them to take their place in the line when their mission on Earth is over.

Every man that has made it this far must now pick up his sword and become Henry V. The landscape is filled with men that are in dire need of what only a dependence on God, reinforced by a warrior culture can do in their lives. Most of them do not realize it, and the rest of them are just waiting on somebody to do it for them. Like Henry V did at Agincourt through a motivational speech, you must do in leading by example.

The ball is in your hands and the clock is ticking down. It is up to you to pray about where God wants you in this battle and then step out on faith and go there. I've given you all of the insight that I have about building an army of dangerous men and forming a Warrior Culture. There are men wandering through life alone that need what only another brother can give him by way of prayers and masculine support. Although most men do not realize it, we are dieing for man to man friendship as a source to draw strength from each other. It's time to start, what are you waiting for?

Epilogue

As a fan of military history, I love to read the
stories of Civil War battles. One of my favorite
battles to study is Gettysburg, especially the well
known failure of Pickett's Charge. On July 3, 1863,
an estimated 12,000 men of the Confederate Army
traveled across open ground with the goal of over-
taking the Union forces dug in atop a small hill
known as Cemetery Ridge. The results were disas-
trous for the Confederates which lost between 50-
60% of their troops.

It must have been sheer terror that engulfed the
minds of these soldiers as they followed orders and
moved across a mile of open ground, taking constant
enemy fire, and seeing the men around them cut to
bits. As heroic as the infantry soldier armed with
his musket was, it occurs to me that the most heroic
person on the battlefield has always been the color
bearer. He selflessly toted the unit flag across the
battlefield, and unarmed I might add.

Color bearers were a special breed of men, vital to every unit. Although they only carried a flag on a pole, they were the symbol of strength and inspiration and their presence alone gave strength to the fighting men around them. The enemy new that killing the color bearer and ultimately capturing the flag was the most demoralizing blow they could give their opponent. So in every battle, each side made sure to target the color bearer.

Given the state of today's men, you must be the color bearer. By taking on this duty, please know that you are charging headlong into a barrage of fire. You will be shot at and possibly wounded by Enemy fire. However, unlike the defenseless Civil War color bearer, you are armed with the armor of God that can deflect the fiery darts that Satan will hurl at you. So be on your guard and expect attacks from the Enemy to come against you, your family, and the men of your group. Identify them for what they are and deflect them with the authority of Christ.

I pray that if you have learned anything from this book, it is that Satan is real and he is out to get you. He will attack you, but you can also expect opposition from other people. I like to call this the human element of attack that is normally carried out against you because of fear. There are many different types of fear involved but the one that I have run into the most is the fear of change. It is an established fact that we are creatures of habit and do not like change of any kind. In fact, the idea of change brings fear into the hearts of many because with any change there is always the unknown wildcard that can only be revealed with the passage of time. Most people that reject a new idea do so because it may alter the way things have "always been done". Let me ask you this, where would we be today if Christopher Columbus had been afraid of the unknown? You may find yourself in a position like Columbus when you begin charting new territory as you set out to change an established institution. Remember the old bumper sticker "God is My Co-Pilot" and believe it. With God plotting the course, His will is going to be done one way or the other. So, expect to raise some eyebrows, both good and bad, of the people around you.

The final prayer that I leave with you is that you persevere. I've laid out how men just don't get it when it comes to the need for other male relationships. The hard part is getting this trend started. If you expect men to drop everything they are doing and join you in your quest, you will be discouraged. You have a daunting task ahead of you. Always be reminded of the fact that this is what God called you to do and he never takes back a calling that he has given out. You are His color bearer.